T0231208

Internet Searching and Indexing:
The Subject Approach

Internet Searching and Indexing: The Subject Approach has been co-published simultaneously as *Journal of Internet Cataloging,* Volume 2, Numbers 3/4 2000.

Internet Searching and Indexing: The Subject Approach

Alan R. Thomas
James R. Shearer
Editors

Internet Searching and Indexing: The Subject Approach has been co-published simultaneously as *Journal of Internet Cataloging,* Volume 2, Numbers 3/4 2000.

CRC Press
Taylor & Francis Group
Boca Raton London New York

CRC Press is an imprint of the
Taylor & Francis Group, an **informa** business

INDEXING & ABSTRACTING

Contributions to this publication are selectively indexed or abstracted in print, electronic, online, or CD-ROM version(s) of the reference tools and information services listed below. This list is current as of the copyright date of this publication. See the end of this section for additional notes.

- *AGRICOLA Database*
- *Applied Social Sciences Index & Abstracts (ASSIA) (Online: ASSI via Data-Star) (CDRom: ASSIA Plus)*
- *BUBL Information Service, an Internet-based Information Service for the UK higher education community <URL: http://bubl.ac.uk/>*
- *Cambridge Scientific Abstracts*
- *CNPIEC Reference Guide: Chinese National Directory of Foreign Periodicals*
- *Combined Health Information Database (CHID)*
- *Computer Literature Index*
- *Current Awareness Abstracts of Library & Information Management Literature, ASLIB (UK)*
- *Current Cites (Digital Libraries) (Electronic Publishing) (Multimedia & Hypermedia) (Networks & Networking) (General)*
- *Current Index to Journals in Education*
- *FINDEX, free Internet Directory of over 150,000 publications from around the world (www.publist.com)*
- *Index to Periodical Articles Related to Law*
- *Information Science Abstracts*
- *INSPEC*
- *Konyvtari Figyelo–Library Review*
- *Library & Information Science Abstracts (LISA)*
- *Library and Information Science Annual (LISCA) (www.lu.com/arba)*
- *Microcomputer Abstracts (www.infotoday.com)*
- *MLA International Bibliography*

(continued)

- *PASCAL, c/o Institute de L'Information Scientifique et Technique. Cross-disciplinary electronic database covering the fields of science, technology & medicine. Also available on CD-ROM, and can generate customized retrospective searches (www.inist.fr)*
- *Referativnyi Zhurnal (Abstracts Journal of the All-Russian Institute of Scientific and Technical Information)*
- *Social Work Abstracts*

Special Bibliographic Notes related to special journal issues (separates) and indexing/abstracting:

- indexing/abstracting services in this list will also cover material in any "separate" that is co-published simultaneously with Haworth's special thematic journal issue or DocuSerial. Indexing/abstracting usually covers material at the article/chapter level.
- monographic co-editions are intended for either non-subscribers or libraries which intend to purchase a second copy for their circulating collections.
- monographic co-editions are reported to all jobbers/wholesalers/approval plans. The source journal is listed as the "series" to assist the prevention of duplicate purchasing in the same manner utilized for books-in-series.
- to facilitate user/access services all indexing/abstracting services are encouraged to utilize the co-indexing entry note indicated at the bottom of the first page of each article/chapter/contribution.
- this is intended to assist a library user of any reference tool (whether print, electronic, online, or CD-ROM) to locate the monographic version if the library has purchased this version but not a subscription to the source journal.
- individual articles/chapters in any Haworth publication are also available through the Haworth Document Delivery Service (HDDS).

Internet Searching and Indexing: The Subject Approach

CONTENTS

Acknowledgments

Having worked previously with Dr. Ruth C. Carter on a special issue of *Cataloging & Classification Quarterly*, we were glad to have the benefit of her experience and suggestions regarding the present collection of papers. The Centre for Information Management, Thames Valley University, London, has made various facilities available to us in our venture.

We thank all the contributors for their papers, which we found purposive, stimulating, thoughtful, and diverse, and we particularly appreciated their patience during a period when both editors were unwell.

Comments and suggestions are welcome and should be sent to the editors at: (alro.th@virgin.net or pjjjf@aol.com).

Alan R. Thomas
James R. Shearer

ABOUT THE EDITORS

Alan R. Thomas, MA, FLA, is Visiting Associate Professor at Pratt Institute, New York, and Visiting Research Fellow at Thames Valley University, London. He has taught at several British and American schools of library and information science, and published many articles and book reviews. He has edited collections in the field of classification and cataloging. He has served on the committees of three controlled vocabularies, and is a member of the editorial board of *Cataloging & Classification Quarterly* (The Haworth Press, Inc.).

James R. Shearer, MA, ALA, is a freelance information consultant and part-time Principal Lecturer in the Centre for Information Management at Thames Valley University, London. He has taught courses on information studies in many countries and has published a number of books, papers, and book reviews. He has designed and developed several thesauri that are in current use.

Introduction:
Increasing the Odds

Alan R. Thomas
James R. Shearer

Je ne cherche pas; je trouve. (attributed to Pablo Picasso)

Fast bind, fast find (William Shakespeare, *The Merchant of Venice*, 1600)

Picasso's strategy might be rendered as "I'll know it when I see it." Information scientists also use this approach but they know it as serendipity–"the faculty of making happy and unexpected discoveries by accident" (Oxford English Dictionary). When it works, it often returns useful results. It cannot, however, be relied on because there is no procedure that can be invoked to guarantee that it will work.

This collection of papers considers the tools and procedures now available or of possible future benefit for searching the Internet more systematically, and also discusses how Internet pages can be modified to facilitate more efficient retrieval.

We hope that the topics treated and the questions posed herein will prove interesting, challenging, and valuable to a wide audience. This audience may include:

Alan R. Thomas is Visiting Associate Professor at Pratt Institute, New York, and Visiting Research Fellow at Thames Valley University, London.

James R. Shearer is a freelance information consultant and part-time Principal Lecturer in the Centre for Information Management at Thames Valley University, London.

[Haworth co-indexing entry note]: "Introduction: Increasing the Odds." Thomas, Alan R., and James R. Shearer. Co-published simultaneously in *Journal of Internet Cataloging* (The Haworth Information Press, an imprint of The Haworth Press, Inc.) Vol. 2, No. 3/4, 2000, pp. 1-5; and: *Internet Searching and Indexing: The Subject Approach* (ed: Alan R. Thomas, and James R. Shearer) The Haworth Information Press, an imprint of The Haworth Press, Inc., 2000, pp. 1-5. Single or multiple copies of this article are available for a fee from The Haworth Document Delivery Service [1-800-342-9678, 9:00 a.m. - 5:00 p.m. (EST). E-mail address: getinfo@haworthpressinc.com].

- Internet users who wish to develop their search skills as well as to gain insight into how indexing and abstracting is done on the Internet
- Front-line library and information professionals–such as reference librarians and readers' advisors–who assist end-users to search Web sites and OPACs
- Professional library catalogers and classifiers and their support staff
- Faculty and students in schools of information and library science, and those who train library staff in electronic database use or provide bibliographic instruction
- Information professionals generally (and managers specifically) who wish to increase their awareness of developments and pitfalls.

Some of the contributions contain information and guidance of value primarily to beginners or relatively inexperienced subject searchers. Other papers should prove thought-provoking and helpful to those with greater experience of subject searching and search tools. Further contributions raise conceptual issues about the organization of knowledge that have serious implications for the subject approach to the Internet.

With the continuous growth of direct searching of the Web with its countless sources from across the world, there is a great need to provide guidance on how to search effectively. These relatively new users–adults and children–are unfamiliar with the highly structured, conceptual modes and beautifully polished abstracts used in traditional hard-copy indexes and bibliographic online databases. These end-users seldom have formal training in the use of libraries, subject bibliographies, indexes, descriptors, abstracts, etc. If in their Internet searching, they happen to meet controlled vocabularies, syntactical subtleties, syndetic relationships, and elaborate hierarchies with chains and ordered arrays, these unfamiliar features are not sufficiently or explicitly highlighted or are forgotten in the mass of detail displayed on the screen.

Information professionals must consider various ways of improving and clarifying users' search experiences so that the yield proves more valuable. The Internet pages of information available to users are constantly growing in number, and the variety and sheer quantity of available and supposedly pertinent pages, records, and links lead to a daunting information overload for both novices and experienced information professionals. The fruits of automatic and human indexing are increasingly available to information professionals and their patrons, so it is appropriate to ponder the precise contribution of each mode of indexing and the relations between them.

Following an *Introduction*, the first section entitled *Search Engines: Characteristics and Effective Use* makes detailed scrutiny of what is currently offered by the search engines, with a range of suggestions on the development or augmentation of these tools. Scott Nicholson anticipates the likely question of "Why not just label anything that helps people search the Internet a 'search engine' and be done with it?" He recognizes many different types of Web search tools, proposes a categorization and nomenclature for the variety, and discusses advantages and disadvantages of each type. He suggests seven questions (including selection and indexing policies) to ask when considering using any Web search tool, for if a searcher believes that search engines are all similarly compiled and indexed, then searching may be poor and inappropriate. Making distinctions would serve also to enhance professional discussion, tuition, and research on Web search tools. Catherine Hume seeks to reach information professionals who are inexperienced Internet users. She gives an overview of the Internet–the "greatest reference tool of the 20th century"–and the Web, Web mastering, and search engines, and aims to show what they can do for an information worker and to answer the echoing question "Where do I start?" Kurt I. Munson then examines critically the automated approach to creating search engines and the implications for searching. He specifies how good searching is a skilled task, one that "is vital for a modern information specialist to acquire and apply." Susan Mac-Dougall asks "What does it matter how relevant or useful information is if it is inaccessible?" She considers a wide variety of helpful signposts to improve access to information on the Web, including browser bookmarks, indexes and directories, temporary search engine results, and metadata. She believes that the rich theory of vocabulary control for online databases can be adapted for Web index construction. Sarah J. Clarke describes, exemplifies, and evaluates recent developments of Web search engines with a view to improving the quality of search results. She notes that the effectiveness of the ranking algorithm in matching Web pages to a query is crucial to user satisfaction.

Next is *Classification and Its Contribution to Web Organization, Indexing, and Searching,* which shows how library and bibliographic classification approaches could enhance Web retrieval. David Ellis and Ana Vasconcelos caution that in today's fast-moving information retrieval world "it is easy to overlook the relevance of classic techniques such as facet analysis." They point out the many benefits of using facet analysis in Web page organization, indexing, and searching. In similar vein, Alan Wheatley believes that "Classification has been important for library-based information retrieval for so long that its particular properties and suitabilities have almost been forgotten." He indicates search limitations of the typical contemporary OPAC, and he shows how and why the popular subject trees on the Internet have adapted principles of conventional bibliographic classification to facilitate information retrieval. Vanda Broughton and Heather Lane confirm the promise of faceted classification as a multi-role Web organizer, and they envisage faceted classification as a "yardstick for the mapping of subject based information across the barriers of language, both natural and index."

Finally, *Subject Cataloguing and the World Wide Web* considers how the Web is and might be used to assist the processes of cataloging and classification. Chris Evin Long acknowledges the "presumptuousness and futility of trying to take aim at such a fast-moving target as Web-based OPAC development." She points out that although users of online catalogs search predominantly by subject, the subject search is the hardest one for them to perform, and observes that the syndetic structure of subject headings is drawn on by only a very few Web-based catalogs to help users plan and modify their searches. She considers the problems of and the potential for improving subject searching in Web-based OPACs, and proposes basic guidelines for interface design. Gordon Dunsire also brings out catalogers' difficulties, noting that even a "trained, professional cataloguer finds it difficult to retrieve from someone else's catalogue." He describes how Scottish and other British catalogers and subject classifiers use the various Internet facilities to help them in their work. William E. Studwell reminds us that the cataloging community bears responsibility for debate and decisions on how to catalog information found on the Internet. He argues that the Internet is an electronic replication of human activity and that the controlled subject vocabulary for it should mirror the world's most used list (Library of Congress subject headings)–"it is not unreasonable for subject access to join the ever expanding club of international cooperation." He proposes and describes a device which would facilitate multinational, multicultural, and multilingual subject access; this device is a three-element punctuation system (dash, equals sign, slash) to represent particular kinds of relationship between terms within a subject string. This system, designed for automated use on the Internet and elsewhere, could be applied to the terms that comprise the Library of Congress subject headings.

These eleven papers taken as a set depict the present state and use of subject indexing and search tools. Further, they offer analyses of principles, techniques, and tools which should prove of transfer value over the longer term in assessing and exploiting future advances. Developments are certain to include greater provision of multifaced search tools, systematic subject order, subject search intermediary facilities (both human and machine), and multicultural perspectives.

SEARCH ENGINES: CHARACTERISTICS AND EFFECTIVE USE

The spider's touch, how exquisitely fine!
Feels at each thread, and lives along the line.

–Alexander Pope, *An Essay on Man,* 1733

The web of our life is of a mingled yarn, good and ill together

–William Shakespeare, *All's Well That Ends Well,* 1602?

A Proposal for Categorization and Nomenclature for Web Search Tools

Scott Nicholson

SUMMARY. Ambiguities in Web search tool (more commonly known as "search engine") terminology are problematic when conducting precise, replicable research or when teaching others to use search tools. Standardized terminology would enable Web searchers to be aware of subtle differences between Web search tools and the implications of these for searching. A categorization and nomenclature for standardized classifications of different aspects of Web search tools is proposed, and advantages and disadvantages of using tools in each category are discussed. *[Article copies available for a fee from The Haworth Document Delivery Service: 1-800-342-9678. E-mail address: getinfo@haworthpressinc.com <Website: http://www.haworthpressinc.com>]*

KEYWORDS. Web search tools, search engines, Web searching, search tool comparisons, Web indexing, Web searching guides, Web searching tutorials

INTRODUCTION AND INSPIRATION

Search engines, search tools, robot-generated databases, Web search services, and Web keyword indexes are all names given to tools

---

Scott Nicholson is an Information Science PhD candidate at the University of North Texas and creator of AskScott.com, virtual reference librarian (snicholson@bigfoot.com).

[Haworth co-indexing entry note]: "A Proposal for Categorization and Nomenclature for Web Search Tools." Nicholson, Scott. Co-published simultaneously in *Journal of Internet Cataloging* (The Haworth Information Press, an imprint of The Haworth Press, Inc.) Vol. 2, No. 3/4, 2000, pp. 9-28; and: *Internet Searching and Indexing: The Subject Approach* (ed: Alan R. Thomas, and James R. Shearer) The Haworth Information Press, an imprint of The Haworth Press, Inc., 2000, pp. 9-28. Single or multiple copies of this article are available for a fee from The Haworth Document Delivery Service [1-800-342-9678, 9:00 a.m. - 5:00 p.m. (EST). E-mail address: getinfo@haworthpressinc.com].

9

that allow searching for and retrieval of World Wide Web sites.[1, 2, 3, 4, 5] As any field develops, the terminology becomes more and more precise. In current Web search tool research, however, there is much imprecision. Not only can this lead to confusion on the part of the reader of this research, but assumptions based on this imprecision can cause researchers to conduct biased or inconsistent studies.

For example, in a recent *Science* article, Lawrence and Giles discuss a group of "full-text search engines."[6] They go on to state that "the Web can be viewed as a searchable 15-billion-word encyclopedia."[7] What problems would it cause if some of the pages of this encyclopedia had every word listed in the index while other pages had only a few selected words listed? In order to successfully find a page, one would have to know what type of indexing was used for it. Several of the "full-text" search tools (e.g., Lycos and HotBot) examined in this research[6] actually do not index the full text of each page. Proper categorization of the search tools would allow researchers to select groups of similar tools for study.

Clark and Willett[8] ran the same searches on three different search tools: AltaVista, Excite, and Lycos. They reported that there were "significant differences between AltaVista and Excite, and between AltaVista and Lycos, but not between Excite and Lycos"[9] and then pointed out the "high level of performance of the AltaVista system."[9] At the time of that research, Excite and Lycos were in one category of search tool (extract search tools), and AltaVista was in a different category (full-text search tools). However, the majority of their queries involved phrases which only the full-text search tools could handle properly. Their research design therefore favors any full-text search tool, such as AltaVista. Clearly, without precise categorization of Web search tools, biases can be unknowingly introduced into the research.

Standardized terminology and categorization also can assist in teaching others how to use search tools effectively. Most books on Internet searching teach how to use AltaVista, Excite, and other specific tools. This method is like teaching users how to use the Oxford English Dictionary, then showing them how to use the Merriam-Webster Dictionary, without telling them what is assumed when one uses that particular dictionary. Categorization allows trainers to teach about a class of search tools and use examples from that group during the lesson, instead of just teaching about individual tools. More importantly, categorization also allows users to understand new or changed tools and modify their searching techniques to fit the tool in question.

SANS "SEARCH ENGINE"

The first problem is what to call the whole group of tools used for Web searching. In the popular culture, "search engine" is the term generally used to describe these tools. However, "search engine" means something different to most information retrieval researchers and has traditionally referred to the programs that do the actual matching of query terms to a database in an IR system. Therefore, many are uncomfortable applying "search engine" to Web directories like Yahoo and other search tools. Using this term can result in unclear communication, and it is suggested that the term "search engine" be avoided in the discussion of these tools.

Instead, to describe the comprehensive class of tools used to search the World Wide Web, the author proposes the use of *Web search tools* or *search tools* for short. This is clear, recognizable, and unambiguous; it also allows the inclusion of tools not yet invented that may not use any type of search engine. Most search tools are made up of several components; these may include the Web robot, a Web page database, a search interface, and Web page surrogates.

PROPOSED CLASSIFICATIONS FOR ASPECTS OF WEB SEARCH TOOLS

Web Robots

The *Web robot* is a program that traverses the World Wide Web, gathering candidates for pages to be indexed in the search tool. Some Web robots visit a page and all linked pages, some visit pages submitted by Web page authors, and others start with "What's New" or "What's Cool" Web pages. These programs are also called[2] spiders, crawlers, and harvesters, among other things, but in order to aid in successful, standardized communication, *Web robot* is the proposed terminology. Some search tools do not use Web robots; a human finds the pages for inclusion in the database, so the candidate pages will be *human-gathered* as compared to *robot-gathered*. A few tools provide access to pages both robot-gathered and human-gathered.

The method of gathering affects the quality of pages available in the database. If humans have gathered the pages, there can be a level of quality control that does not exist in the robot-gathered Web search tools. However, the robot-gathered Web search tools may be more methodological in gathering all of the pages in a Web site (if programmed that way) and will gather more pages overall than a human. Therefore, human-gathered Web search tools can provide higher-quality Web sites for searching, and robot-gathered Web search tools will most likely provide a larger quantity of Web sites to search.

Web Page Databases

Information retrieved by the Web robot is then put into a *Web page database* (the word "page" is used in order to distinguish this from databases of material that are Web-accessible). Most Web page databases consist of indexes and related surrogates. Knowing certain aspects of the Web page database index is the key to selection and proper use of the appropriate search tool for a specific search request;[10] however, most articles on Web search tools in the popular media compare only the search interfaces.

Topicality of Web Page Databases

Some databases contain records only on a specific subject such as health or business. These come in many different forms but will all be called *subject-specific* search tools, while tools that collect data on a variety of topics will be called *general* search tools. Most of the commonly discussed search tools are general search tools (such as AltaVista, Excite, and Hotbot); however, the rewards of finding and using a subject-specific search tool will be discussed later in this article.

Method of Indexing Used

One aspect of Web page databases is the method used to index retrieved Web pages. The information collected by a Web robot may be presented to a person for review, or the human that gathers the page may also index it. In either case it will be termed a *manually indexed*

Web page database. These databases may consist of keywords and/or controlled vocabulary selected from the Web page and short abstracts or reviews of the page. If the Web robot works with another computer program to process the information without human intervention, it is an *automatically-indexed* Web page database.

In automatically-indexed Web page databases, there is an important distinction to make. Some Web page databases contain every word from every page indexed, and are called *full-text* search tools. Other tools index every word on the page except for a list of stopwords, and these are called *full-text without stopwords* search tools. A third class of tools contain Web page databases made up of automatically selected extracts (the first n words, the most frequently used words, or words from the title or headers) from each Web page. These are called *extracting* search tools. The distinction between indexing methods is very important. Knowing the form of indexing used helps the searcher determine what topics will be easily searchable and what types of search strategies may be effective.[10]

Full-Text Search Tools (AltaVista, Infoseek)

These tools attempt to be the most comprehensive Web search tools by indexing the full text of every page included in the Web page database. Because of the full-text indexing, these search tools can be challenging to use for the novice searcher; they tend to overwhelm the user with results. The relevance ranking algorithm used in these tools can bring some useful pages to the top of the list; however, unscrupulous Web designers search for ways to design their pages so that they rise to the top, regardless of the usefulness of their content.

While a user might imagine that the full-text search tools provide a comprehensive listing of Web pages, this is not the case. Not only is each one linked to a different Web page database, each indexes a different part of the Web. In fact, even the largest tools index no more than (and probably considerably less than) 35% of the Web.[6] Therefore, if a high-recall, comprehensive search is desired, a user must search using all tools available and be prepared to follow links from pages to discover pages not indexed in any Web searching tool.

Full-Text Without Stopwords Search Tools (Excite, Hotbot)

These tools index every word on every page in their database with the exception of stopwords, such as and, or, not, the, and other common words. To the unsuspecting searcher, these tools act like the full-text search tools. However, if a searcher tries to find a phrase containing stopwords, such as "To be or not to be," they will have difficulties. For this reason, it is important to distinguish between these two types of full-text search tool.

Extracting Search Tools (Lycos)

These tools will usually provide fewer pages on a topic than either type of the full-text search tools. As these tools do not index every word on the page, many of the techniques used to limit the output described above will not work. For example, the lack of phrase searching with these tools can make it difficult to achieve a high level of precision. However, if the search topic is general, if there are not any applicable phrases that might appear on all the target pages, or if the search terms tend to be used out-of-context, these tools may provide better results than a full-text tool.

When reading older research, it is useful to know that Excite used to be an extracting search tool, and now is a full-text without stopwords search tool. However, this change was not announced; it just happened one day. Thus, as a researcher, it is worth checking the help screens on search tools every so often to catch significant changes like this.

SEARCH INTERFACES

The *search interface* is the method that allows the user to extract information from the Web page database. Although most Web page databases have only one interface attached to them, a few search tools allow different methods of accessing the same database. The two types of interfaces currently available are query boxes and subject trees.

Query Box

A *query box* accepts free-text from the user and extracts records from the Web page database via a matching and ranking algorithm. Query boxes can link into automatically-indexed or manually-indexed Web page databases. A user will type in *search terms* (words representing the different facets of the search) and can use *operators*. The operators available may be Boolean connectors, term weighting, grouping, or some of each. *Boolean* operators may include AND, OR, NOT, AND NOT, and truncation. One caveat with Boolean is that these operators do not always mean what they have meant in traditional types of searching. The AND, for example, may be a "fuzzy AND," where first all items containing both search terms are returned, and then items containing one or the other are returned. The only place to learn the meanings of the Boolean terms used is the help screens attached to the search tool.

Term weighting operators are symbols like + or − entered directly before a search term. The plus sign usually means that items must have that search term to be returned (i.e., very high term weight), while the minus sign means that items with that search term will not be returned or be returned at the bottom of the list and thus have a very low term weight.

Grouping operators are symbols like " ". The quotes are used for phrase searching and are the most powerful tool in the searcher's arsenal. Apart from obvious cases, such as proper nouns or lines from poems or songs, phrases can be used to find factual answers easily when a full-text index is accessed through the interface. In the future, search tools may offer other grouping modifiers like those found in DIALOG (NEAR, WITH).

Another issue to consider is the *default operator.* When a searcher does not enter any operator, the search tool uses some type of default. This is important to consider in Web search tool research and controlling variables. Some search tools default to AND, some default to OR, some default to a "fuzzy AND" (where they do an AND and then an OR), and some just have the defaults built into their relevance ranking algorithms.

When entering terms without using any connectors in many search tools, the user can gain more precise results by entering more terms. However, if more synonyms are entered for one search facet than another facet, pages matching more of the synonyms for that facet may be placed higher on the list. This may produce a desired effect or may create a failed search, depending upon the situation. Thus, the user needs to be aware of this quirk/feature.

Subject Tree

A *subject tree* allows the user to select from a hierarchical menu of categories. These lists are almost always created by humans, and thus have all of the problems with human indexing that have been faced in libraries for years. These interfaces are usually linked into manually-indexed Web page databases.

Given that these search tools are usually smaller and manually indexed, there is a level of quality control that does not exist in the automatically-indexed search tools. These are the only search tools good for browsing, as the subject tree interface allows users to look around the Web without a specific topic in mind. The subject tree allows users to wander from topic to topic, finding things they would never have known to look for. It is the closest there is on the Internet to simulating the "shelf browsing" experience in a library.

If the topic is general and there is a heading for that topic, a subject tree is the best place to start research. One can begin to see the type of information existing on the Web for that topic, and may be able learn how pages in that field are organized. Compared to results from a general topic search in an automatically-indexed tool, the resulting list of Web sites will be short (perhaps too short); however, users generally will not feel inundated with hits.

Even if there is not a heading for the general topic in question, a tool based on a subject tree (such as Yahoo) may be used to find a few pages on the topic if the tool has a query box. Many times, once a user finds one good page on a topic, links on that page can be followed for further information on that topic. The chances of finding a relevant starting point with a subject tree are better because of the human intervention.

It is important to specify the type of search interfaces and modifiers available with the search tool so that a search can be planned. For example, a user who wants to find a song lyric will have much better luck using a full-text search tool that has a query box that allows grouping. If the user wants to be able to jump to a short listing of pages on a general topic, then the user needs a Web search tool with both a subject tree and a query box. In Web tool research, it is essential to acknowledge what type of search interface and modifiers are used in order for the study to be replicable.

After accepting the search, the search interface uses a *matching and ranking algorithm* which will find pages that match the user's search terms under the constraints of the connectors and will produce a list of references to Web pages. This list, called a *result set*, will usually be ordered by a descending *relevance score*, which rates the similarity between the search and the Web page assigned to each Web page database entry by the algorithm. These algorithms are guarded by the companies, as unscrupulous site designers will attempt to figure out how best to manipulate their page to end up near the top of the list.

Because the matching and ranking algorithms are held secret, Web search tool research usually requires a black box approach. Queries are dropped into the black box, and results come out the other side. Other aspects of the Web search tools can be learned and thus controlled. While research that compares Web search tools can control for many aspects of the search; however, the effectiveness of the matching and ranking algorithms will always be a point of variance.

Web Page Surrogates

Just as a card in the card catalog represents a book in the library, the *Web page surrogate* is a representation of a Web page. Web page surrogates are presented to the user in response to a query, and may or may not be the same as the Web page database entry used for matching a query. This can be frustrating for the user who does not know this, as they cannot determine why a page was returned from the Web page surrogate.

These surrogates are made up of a *citation* and an *abstract*. The citation usually is the relevance score, the title of the page, the URL, and other information about the page. One important piece of information in many surrogate citations is the *refresh date*. This date is the last time the Web search tool visited the Web page. These, along with dead links, can be an indicator of a Web search tool that is not kept up-to-date.

There are different types of abstracts available. If the Web page database is full-text, the abstract may be a *context abstract*, which presents the parts of the Web page with the words in context, or a *standard abstract*, which will usually consist of the first few lines of the Web page. However, if the Web page databases are indexed only by keywords, then there will be only a standard abstract available. A *brief abstract* contains the title and URL of the page, and possibly a few words about the content of the page (created automatically or by humans).

Here are examples of each type of abstract for the same Web page:

Brief abstract (from www.go.com's Topics):
AskScott: Your guide to finding it on the Internet
Virtual reference librarian recommends search tools for specific types of searches. http://www.askscott.com/

Standard Abstract (from www.altavista.com):
AskScott–Your guide to finding it on the Internet.
Need Help? I'm Scott, the Virtual Reference Librarian. As you are answering questions on the right, look at this column to get advice, commentary, or see . . .
URL: askscott.com/
Last modified 20-May-99–page size 4K–in English [*Translate*]

Context Abstract (from www.google.com):
AskScott–Your guide to finding it on the Internet.
. . . other options: * Orientation to *AskScott* * Searching . . .
. . . stocks > Something else What is *AskScott*? Just as the reference . . .
www.askscott.com/ *Cached (4k)*

In some search tools, the user can choose the type of information provided in the Web page surrogate. If this is possible, it is important to note what types of surrogates are examined in a Web search tool study. If the study uses selection of pages from a result set, the type of abstract presented may change the selections made by the subject. If relevance judgments are going to be made directly from the search results screen, then the type of surrogate examined will have great effect on the study. Being aware of the different types of surrogates allows the researcher to control for bias that might be introduced by comparing different types of surrogates.

Other Parts

Most Web search tools have all or most of these four parts. However, there are some parts not listed here which exist only in a few tools. One of these is Excite's "More Like This" feature; it allows a user to re-define a search based on characteristics (chosen by Excite) of a seed document. A similar tool is Lycos's WiseWire addition, which watches a search and makes adjustments based on searcher feedback. These *feedback* mechanisms, if developed and properly advertised, may become a popular and useful feature. It is important to recognize if these are being used in a Web tool study, as they can bias the results if they are used but not reported.

Meta-Search Tools (Inference Find, Dogpile, Metacrawler)

The most problematic yet very popular tool is the *meta-search tool*. These search tools have a search interface, which accepts a query from a user, may or may not translate it, and submits it to several other search tools. The returned surrogates are collected and organized for display. The problem in defining meta-search tools is that they combine the results from searching different types of Web page databases through different interfaces, and the surrogates will come from a variety of ranking and matching algorithms. Because of this chaotic variety, it is difficult to perform precise, controlled searches with these tools.

Summary of Classification

In summary, here are the questions to ask when examining a Web search tool:

1. Are the pages gathered from the Web by robots, humans, or both?
2. Does the Web page database contain pages on a specific subject or is it more general?
3. Are the entries in the Web page database automatically indexed or manually indexed?
4. Is the full text or only portions from each page indexed for the Web page database? Is there a list of stopwords that the index does not include?
5. Does the Web search tool have a subject tree or query box interface?
   a. If it has a query box interface, what operators does it allow?
6. Are the returned abstracts based on the context in which the terms appear, or are they standardized or brief abstracts?
7. Is it a Meta-search tool?

IMPLICATIONS FOR CLASSIFICATION

Once the aspects of a Web search tool have been classified, the searcher can have a better idea of what type of search will be successful there. Conversely, if the searcher has a query in mind, s/he can select the most appropriate search tool for that query. This is the concept behind AskScott (http://www.askscott.com), where the user is asked questions about a query and directed to the most appropriate search tool.

CATEGORIES FOR WEB SEARCH TOOLS

Five categories (Table 1) are suggested based upon the above terminology, although new categories can be created as needed. Each category involves one or more assumptions about aspects of search tools. When an assumption is not met, then the area of difference should be specified when discussing the search tool. For example, a directory-based search tool that is on a specific topic would be referred to as a subject-specific directory-based search tool, but a directory-based search tool that is general would need no additional qualifiers.

Directory-Based Search Tools (Yahoo, Looksmart, About.Com)

These are tools based on a subject tree search interface. The pages may be gathered by Web robots or humans, but the pages are indexed by humans. The surrogates, usually brief abstracts, are organized in a subject tree, although some tools have a query box as well. When there is a query box and a subject tree that search the same directory, any controls placed upon use need to be stated in Web tool research.

Full-Text Search Tools (AltaVista, Excite, Infoseek)

Search tools that automatically index every word on every Web page are called full-text search tools. These have pages gathered by robots, although users can suggest pages for the robots to visit. The search interface is a query box that allows a combination of Boolean and term weighting connectors, including the phrase connector. The abstracts are usually standardized, although the user may have a choice of abstract format.

Also included in this category are the full-text without stopwords search tools. In most respects, they can be used in the same way as the full-text search tools. However, when phrase searching, it is important to remember that full-text without stopwords search tools will produce poor results if stopwords are in the phrase used for searching.

Extracting Search Tools (Lycos, Webcrawler)

In comparison to the full-text search tools, extracting search tools automatically index only parts of the Web pages. In some cases, they index only the title, headings and first 100 words. In other cases, they index the most commonly used words. These tools tend to be targets for dishonest Web-page designers who learn their indexing methods and exploit them. Other than the difference in indexing, these tools created are just like full-text search tools. Some even allow limited phrase searching, although it will not be as useful in an extracting search tool as it is with a full-text search tool as any phrase containing a term not indexed from the Web page will fail to find that page.

Subject-Specific Search Tools (Achoo, Mutual Funds Online, HomeArts Network)

The only thing these tools have in common is that the Web page database contains records on a given topic. Each one of these tools is different, and very few of them offer the variety of search options that the larger general tools offer. However, if there is a subject-specific search tool available, searching on the subject will be much less frustrating and faster than searching with a general search tool. It can be difficult to locate these subject-specific search tools but there are resources such as http://www.search.com, http://www.ipl.org/ref/, or http://www.clearinghouse.net that are lists of these tools.

Meta-Search Tools (Inference Find, Dogpile, Metacrawler)

The most problematic yet very popular tool is the *meta-search tool.* These search tools have a search interface, which accepts a query from a user, may or may not translate it, and submits it to several other search tools. The returned surrogates are collected and organized for display. The problem in defining meta-search tools is that they combine the results from searching different types of Web page databases through different interfaces, and the surrogates will come from a variety of ranking and matching algorithms. Because of this chaotic variety, it is difficult to perform precise, controlled searches with these tools.

TABLE 1. Categories of Web Search Tools

Type of search tool	Assumptions made
Directory-based search tool	Manually indexed Web page database General Web page database Subject tree search interface Brief abstracts
Full-text search tool	Robot-gathered Web page database General Web page database Automatically-indexed Web page database Full-text index (with or without stopwords) Phrase searching allowed Query box search interface Standard abstracts
Extracting search tool	Robot-gathered Web page database General Web page database Automatically-indexed Web page database No phrase searching Keyword index Query box search interface Standard abstracts
Subject-specific search tool	All pages in the Web page database are related to a specific subject Human-gathered Web page database
Meta-search tool	Searches other Web search tools and combines the results General Web page database Query box search interface

ADVANTAGES AND DISADVANTAGES OF TOOLS FROM DIFFERENT CATEGORIES

Different categories of Web search tools are useful for different tasks. Just as one would not use an encyclopedia to look up the definition of a word, one would not use a directory search tool to find the source of a quotation. By knowing the advantages and disadvantages of each category of search tool, the user can select the best search tool for a particular query. As new search tools become available, users can also categorize them and predict what type of searches will be successful.

Directory-Based Search Tools

Given that directory-based search tools are usually smaller and manually indexed, there is a level of quality control that does not exist in the automatically-indexed search tools. These are the only search tools good for browsing, as the subject tree interface allows users to look around the Web without having a specific topic in mind. The directory-based search tools allow users to wander from topic to topic, finding things they would not otherwise have known to look for. It is the closest there is on the Internet to simulating the "shelf browsing" experience in a library.

If the topic is general and there is a directory listing for that topic, a directory-based search tool is the best place to start research. One can begin to see the type of information existing on the Web for that topic, and may be able learn how pages in that field are organized. Compared to results from a general topic search in other categories of search tools, the resulting list of Web sites will be short (perhaps too short); however, users generally will not feel inundated with too many hits.

Even if there is not a heading for the general topic in question, a directory-based tool may be used to find a few pages on the topic if the tool has a query box. Many times, once a user finds one good page on a topic, links on that page can be followed for further information on that topic. The chances of finding a relevant starting point with a directory-based search tool are better because of the human intervention.

The main disadvantage to a directory-based search tool is its size. For example, as of this writing, Yahoo has about 1 million entries while AltaVista has over 140 million.[11,12] They are many times smaller than search tools created automatically, and thus if they do not adequately answer the user's questions, the user will have to either use another search tool or find some pages with links to other pages.

Full-Text Search Tools

The key to using a full-text search tool is the phrase connector. Usually indicated by quotation marks, a phrase search helps users narrow their results and raise their searching precision. For example, the phrases allow users to find all instances of a single form of a person's name or a company in the indexed Web pages. If the person or company is well-known, a directory-based search tool may give more accurate results. But for most identity searches, the full-text search tools will give good results. If there is more than one entity with the same name, placing the term weighting connector to require a term (usually "+") in front of the name and adding a place or topic related to the person can help bring the desired results to the top.

Quotations, song lyrics, and poetry can also be found with the phrase connector. For example, only tools that index every word on the page (including common stop words like the, be, to, or, and, not, etc.) can find the phrase "To be or not to be." As with most Web searching, careful attention should be paid to the authority of the source. Many people, for example, will attach a favorite line from a poem or quotation to a Web page. While personal home pages may provide some information about a quotation, printed resources may need to be consulted if an authoritative answer is needed.

Specific topics, acronyms, and any unique phrases will aid in the precision of a search with the full-text search tool. If there is some specific item that appears somewhere in the body of the Web page, it can be included in quotes when searching. One example of this is in answering factual questions. If the user can conceive of a phrase that would exist on the perfect Web page that would contain an answer to the question, then the user can enter that phrase in quotes. For example, if the question is, "What is the capital of Zimbabwe," the perfect Web page to answer the question might say, "The capital of Zimbabwe is. . . ." Therefore, the search to enter is "capital of Zimbabwe is" in a full-text search tool. Again, the authority of these answers should be examined closely.

It is important to be aware when using a full-text search tool that doesn't index stopwords. As discussed earlier, these tools can be used like the full-text search tools with one exception—phrase searching with a stopword will fail. If users are not aware of this, they may get frustrated when they cannot find "Gone with the Wind," for example. DIALOG makes up for this with the NEAR connector, but so far, Web search tools do not allow the use of this connector. Other than that, searching in these tools is identical to searching the full-text tools.

Extracting Search Tools

These tools are a good second choice after trying either directory-based search tools or full-text search tools. They will provide more results than directory-based tools, although they may still overwhelm the user with results. They will usually provide fewer results than a full-text search tool because only selected parts of the target pages are indexed. The lack of phrase searching with these tools makes it difficult to achieve a high level of precision. However, if the search topic is general, if there are not any applicable phrases that might appear on all the target pages, or if the search terms tend to be used out-of-context, these tools may provide better results than a full-text tool.

Some extracting search tools index the text of the page excluding stop words and therefore any phrase searching allowed will be limited. Many of the comments regarding phrase searching from the full-text search tools section will be applicable here. However, a search including any of the stop words will fail to retrieve pertinent pages.

When entering terms without using any connectors in extract search tools, the user can gain more precise results by entering more terms. However, if more synonyms are entered for one search facet than another facet, pages matching more of the synonyms for that facet may be placed higher on the list. This may produce a desired effect or may lower the ranking of desired pages, depending upon the situation. Thus, the user needs to be aware that entering more synonyms will weight the search toward that facet.

Subject-Specific Search Tools

The advantage to subject-specific search tools is that searching done with them can be very precise, assuming the search tool covers the desired topic. There are full-text and extract subject-specific search tools, as well as subject-specific directory-based search tools. If comprehensive searching is desired, the searcher may want to see if a subject-specific search tool exists before using the general search tools.

Meta-Search Tools

Many people prefer the meta-search tools, as they allow searching in a number of Web page databases at once. The problem with these tools is a lack of control. It is difficult to use connectors properly when searching directory-based tools, extract search tools, and full-text search tools simultaneously, as different tools do different things with connectors. Many of these tools present only the first few pages returned by each search tool; therefore, the performance with these tools varies considerably.

These tools can be good for a "quick and dirty" search, in order to learn what types of pages are on the Internet. Since different search tools tend to index different types of pages, by examining the first few returned pages from a number of search tools, a searcher can use a meta-search tool to decide on which search tools to pursue in-depth searching.

Some of the meta-search tools such as Inference Find, http://www.infind.com, group the returned results by topic instead of by type. This is useful in quickly identifying aspects of a search term that create false drops. After examining the topic categories returned in a search, the searcher can use NOT or "-" to remove groups of pages from the returned list.

CONCLUSION

Why go to all this trouble? Why not just label anything that helps people search the Internet a "search engine" and be done with it? There are differences in the Web page databases that cause problems for the unknowing searcher. Successful queries with one tool may be unsuccessful with another type of tool. This categorization structure brings to light these hidden differences, as summarized in Table 2.

When doing research on Web search tools, care should be taken to compare tools from the same category using the same queries. Using search tools from different categories with the same queries may introduce bias toward certain categories of tools into the research results.

Different types of Web search tools perform better in different circumstances. Regardless of how the users enter the query, if the wrong search tool has been selected, users will get poor results. If users are familiar with the five broad categories of tools and when to use them, they will be better searchers. Thus, when training users (in person or through educational Web sites), the use of this categorization will help to search the Web more successfully.

Finally, by moving away from the ambiguous "search engine" and moving toward more precise terminology, discussion and research in this field will become more precise, replicable, and less confusing.

TABLE 2. Advantages and Disadvantages of Categories of Web Search Tools

Type of tool	Advantages	Sample tools
Directory-based search tool	Browsing Starting point for searching Not as intimidating for novices	http://www.yahoo.com http://www.about.com http://www.looksmart.com
Full-text search tool	Specific companies or people Quotes, poems, or lyrics Specific topic searching "Ready reference" fact searching	http://www.altavista.digital.com http://www.infoseek.com http://www.excite.com
Extracting search tool	Good secondary tool General topic searching Search terms commonly used out-of-context	http://www.lycos.com http://www.webcrawler.com http://www.hotbot.com
Subject-specific search tool	More precise when applicable	http://www.search.com http://www.clearinghouse.net http://www.ipl.org/ref/
Meta-search tool	"Quick and dirty" searching Overview of topic area	http://www.infind.com http://www.dogpile.com http://www.metacrawler.com

REFERENCES

1. Xiaoying Dong and Louise T. Su, "Search Engines on the World Wide Web and Information Retrieval from the Internet: A Review and Evaluation," *Online & CDROM Review* 21:2 (1997): 67-81.

2. Venkat N. Gudivada, Vijay V. Raghavan, William I. Grosky, and Rajesh Kasanagottu, "Information Retrieval on the World Wide Web," *IEEE Internet Computing* 1:5 (1997): 58-68.

3. Stacy Kimmel, "Robot-Generated Databases on the World Wide Web," *Database* 19:1 (1996): 40-49.

4. Wei Ding and Gary Marchionini, "A Comparative Study of Web Search Service Performance," in *Global Complexity: Information, Chaos, and Control, Proceedings of the 59th Annual Meeting of the American Society for Information Science*, Steve Hardin, ed. (Medford, NJ: Information Today, 1996): 136-140.

5. Greg R. Notess, "Searching the World-Wide Web: Lycos, WebCrawler and More," *Online* 19:4 (1995): 48-53.

6. Steve Lawrence and C. Lee Giles, "Searching the World Wide Web," *Science* 280 (1998): 98-100.

7. as 6. p. 98.

8. Sarah J. Clarke and Peter Willett, "Estimating the Recall Performance of Web Search Engines," *Aslib Proceedings* 49:7 (1997): 184-189.

9. as 8. p. 187.

10. Scott Nicholson, "Indexing and Abstracting on the World Wide Web: An Examination of Six Web Page Databases," *Information Technology and Libraries* 16:2 (1997): 73-81.

11. Danny Sullivan, "Search Engine Sizes," <http://www.searchenginewatch.com/reports/sizes.html> (January 1999) Seen 8 January 1999.

12. Danny Sullivan, "Directory Sizes," <http://www.searchenginewatch.com/reports/directories.html> (November 1998) Seen 8 January 1999.

Internet Search Engines and Robots: What They Are and How to Use Them

Catherine Hume

SUMMARY. An overview of the Internet is provided. It describes what the Internet is, how and when it was started, and the four main functions it currently offers. It then focuses on the World Wide Web, and in particular robots and search engines. An overview is provided of both robots and search engines, with some examples and illustrations. It concludes with how to choose a search engine for a particular enquiry, gives some hints and tips for Internet searches, and emphasises that good retrieval is achieved not only by good search engines but also by responsible Web mastering which helps to disseminate effectively any Internet published material. *[Article copies available for a fee from The Haworth Document Delivery Service: 1-800-342-9678. E-mail address: getinfo@haworthpressinc.com <Website: http://www.haworthpressinc.com>]*

KEYWORDS. Internet, World Wide Web, robots, search engines, Web mastering, information retrieval

INTRODUCTION

This article is designed for library and information professionals who have never used the Internet before, or are infrequent or novice

Catherine Hume is Deputy Librarian, Ove Arup Partnership, 36-38 Fitzroy Square, London W1P 5LL, England (c.hume@lbs.ac.uk).

[Haworth co-indexing entry note]: "Internet Search Engines and Robots: What They Are and How to Use Them." Hume, Catherine. Co-published simultaneously in *Journal of Internet Cataloging* (The Haworth Information Press, an imprint of The Haworth Press, Inc.) Vol. 2, No. 3/4, 2000, pp. 29-45; and: *Internet Searching and Indexing: The Subject Approach* (ed: Alan R. Thomas, and James R. Shearer) The Haworth Information Press, an imprint of The Haworth Press, Inc., 2000, pp. 29-45. Single or multiple copies of this article are available for a fee from The Haworth Document Delivery Service [1-800-342-9678, 9:00 a.m. - 5:00 p.m. (EST). E-mail address: getinfo@haworthpressinc.com].

users. Once you have the equipment, browsing the Internet is straight-forward, but it is much like walking into a library and just wandering around hoping you will find the information you are looking for. As information professionals we are charged with the responsibility of knowing our sources and being able to answer queries efficiently and effectively.

The Internet is the largest reference work in the 20th Century. Search engines, directories, robots, spiders, worms, Web crawlers, agents and Web ants are all tools that help us find our way in its labyrinth of information. The object of this article is to provide an answer to that echoing question "where do I start?" It concentrates on the software involved in finding information on the Internet and in the process provides an overview of the Internet, the World Wide Web, browsers, robots, search engines, Meta search engines, how to choose a search engine, getting the most from your search and the responsibility of the Web Master.

This paper resulted from a book review I wrote for the Library Association Information Technology Group Newsletter (ITs News) on *The Library and Information Professional's Guide to the Internet.*[1] In that review I said that "the balance of the book was good except I would have liked more of a review of the various search engines available on the Internet. . . . Being able to differentiate between Yahoo and AltaVista or Web Crawler, knowing what they have to offer and what they will help you find would have been so useful."[2] Everyone who has read this paper will start using the Web armed with a little knowledge of what it offers, thus opening doors to one of the greatest and most fun information resources of our time.

BACKGROUND

Overview of the Internet

The Internet, like other elements of American information infra-structure, was originally conceived by the military as a development of the Cold War. The RAND Corporation was given the task of devising a communications system that would continue to function if a substantial portion of it were to be destroyed. Such a structure needed to be de-centralised, self-monitoring, and failsafe.

The solution devised was a network of linked computers with equal authority to send, pass, and receive messages. The messages themselves were split up into 'packets' consisting of units of data which were addressed to the recipient computer. The exact route that each packet took from the sender to receiver was variable and not dependent on one conduit. Therefore, if part of the network was destroyed, the packets would simply take another route to their destination using the remaining network links. In other words, the packets are sent along a network of networks, finding their way with a range of possible links to their destination.

This 'network of networks' infrastructure was then adopted by Advanced Research Projects Agency Network (ARPANET) in 1969, and throughout the '70s additional networks were developed and linked to one another by gateways. The introduction, in the United Kingdom of the Joint Academic Network (JANET) in 1984 and of the National Science Foundation Network (NSFNET) in the USA in 1986 laid the ground work for what we know today as the Internet. This loose coalition of networks, all linked together by gateways, now supports millions of users world wide. The decentralised structure means no one is directly responsible for monitoring its growth, content or direction. There is no restriction on who can use the Internet. The only limitations to use are (1) obtaining the hardware involved in getting connected, and (2) finding an Internet Service Provider (ISP) to create an account for you and connect the two sets of necessary software. The consequence of this phenomenal success and unstructured growth has been to increase bandwidth, that is, to make the switches and cables capable of handling more traffic and increase the capacity or amount of data that can travel over the network at a given time. Whether this solution can go on indefinitely before the Net grinds to a complete halt is open to question.

That is a little bit on how the Internet works, but what does it offer? Searching for information is only one of several facilities available. Others include e-mail, newsgroups, relay chat, telnet, ftp, and most importantly for us, the World Wide Web. All of the above require specialist software which can be obtained individually or in a cluster with Internet browsers.

Briefly e-mail is like the telephone but in writing. It can be thought of as electronic letters but is much better. An advantage of e-mail over every other form of communication is that it is distance independent.

It costs as much to send an e-mail next door as it does to Australia and unlike the telephone, two way communication takes place at the participants' convenience so you don't end up playing telephone tag trying to get in touch with someone.

Newsgroups or USENET enables people of like minds to group together and create a multi-megabyte discussion forum. Within the newsgroup one person can write simultaneously to everyone who has subscribed to that newsletter.

Internet relay chat permits you to talk to thousands of complete strangers either in a group or individually through a channel. It is a little like short wave radio communication but using a keyboard.

Telnet provides a bridge from one computer to another. This is particularly useful for gaining access to OPACs, library catalogues held on library computers.

File Transfer Protocol (ftp) enables users to download programs available on the Internet. There is a lot of free software available on the Internet, and ftp permits you to transfer it to your computer. In fact all the software needed to run e-mail, newsgroups, etc., is available free on the Internet and ftp helps you to transfer it.

Lastly the World Wide Web (WWW) contains a great fund of information, graphics, audio, and video, all linked together with hypertext links, and serviced by search engines and robots.

The WWW

The concept was invented in 1989 by Tim Berners-Lee, a communications specialist at the European Particle Physics laboratory at CERN in Geneva. He devised an information system using hypertext links which permitted CERN researchers to share their results as quickly as possible over the Internet. The hypertext links used to navigate through the information allowed text to be linked via keywords or phrases to other documents elsewhere on the Internet, all by the simple click of a mouse.

At first, the Web was used only as an experimental tool for exchanging text based information, but the development of browsers such as Netscape and Mosaic enabled people to publish and view Web documents in a rich variety of media such as graphics, sound, and video. The underlying structure which Berners-Lee used for authoring his hypertext linked documents became known as Hypertext Markup Language (HTML), the programming language used for creating Internet Web pages. The great success of the Web lies in the freedom of access, wealth of information, simplicity in creation and use, plus the variety of media it presents. Not only is it useful and simple, but Web pages move, look good, and are in the public domain where anyone can use the information, graphics and data supplied by the pages as they wish.

Browsers

Retrieval capabilities on the WWW have been greatly improved by Internet Browsers. As mentioned above they helped provide access to graphics, sound, and video. In addition it is now possible to get virtually all the software necessary to access every Internet facility (e.g., e-mail, ftp, etc.) in one package. You need a browser in order to access the WWW. 'How to choose the best browser' is the theme of endless literature in Internet journals, discussions among users, and even court cases involving Microsoft and the US government. The two major contenders are Netscape and Microsoft Internet Explorer. They both do the job of searching the Web, and even established computer magazines, such as *PC Computing*, declared a draw between the two.[3] The one you choose will probably be determined by your IT support, and currently both browsers are free, so there is even less to choose between the two of them. Personally I prefer Netscape, perhaps because it was the first one I used. I particularly like the way it structures the bookmarks (stored addresses of useful sites), and I find the extensive history facility (a list of sites you have been to recently) useful when searching.

ROBOTS, SEARCH ENGINES AND MUCH MORE

Robots

The name robot comes from the word in Karel Capek's play of 1921 'R.U.R' for Rossum's Universal Robots, 'robota' being Czech for work.[4] Within the context of the WWW, a robot is a program that automatically traverses the Web's hypertext structure by capturing a document, and recursively retrieving all documents that are referenced. The robot can index any one or a combination of sources. Such sources include the titles of documents, keywords from the text, and Uniform Resource Locators (URLs)–the long Internet address which usually begins http://. . . . A robot visits WWW sites, requests documents, examines the links to that document, and indexes what it finds.

Don't confuse robots with browsers–they are quite different. Web browsers are operated by a human being and do not automatically retrieve linked documents. Robots and their relatives may also be called spiders, worms, Web crawlers, and Web ants, which are often the same but sometimes slightly different. Spider is just another name for robot. Web crawlers are also the same as robots. Web Crawler is the name of a specific robot. Worms are similar, except that a worm is a replicating program, and can be as pernicious as a virus, by getting out of control and tying up hundreds of computers at one time, though this is less of a problem now than in the early days of robots. Lastly, Web ants are distributed co-operating robots. Important things to remember about robots are that they are computer programs, operate automatically, and retrieve and index information.[5]

How does a robot automatically collect the data? This depends on the robot. Each one uses a different strategy, which is why the robots' indexes or databases do not necessarily duplicate each other. Therefore it is worthwhile visiting different search engines which use robots to harvest their databases–more about that later. In general they start from an historical list of URLs such as 'What's New' pages and popular Web sites. In addition, most search engines which use robots also allow the manual submission of URLs. Such registered URLs are then put in a queue and the search engine will then visit the site automatically.[6] To facilitate this process of submitting a URL to an indexing service from a newly created Web site, some general rules, clearly laid out, have been established for the registration.[7]

Here is an example of the type of HTML code you will need to insert at the top of each page, after <HTML> and before <BODY>:

```
<HEAD>
<TITLE>Title for this site. Add a short sentence describing the
site. INCLUDE KEYWORDS IN CAPITALS.</TITLE>
<META NAME= "description" Content="DESCRIPTION OF
YOUR SITE IN CAPITALS.
WE SPECIALIZE IN KEYWORDS FOR YOUR SITE.">
<META NAME = "keywords" Content="LONGER LIST OF
```

KEYWORDS FOR THIS PAGE WITH NO OR MINIMAL
REPETITION">
<META NAME="revisit-after" CONTENT="15 days">
<META NAME="ROBOTS" CONTENT="ALL">
</HEAD>

Now apply the rules[7] to the outline HTML material above:

Rule 1: Every page on your site must have the >HEAD> . . . </HEAD> code.

Rule 2: Give every page a title. This should be limited to 20 words maximum, and should be enough to entice people onto your site. It's all that they will see in the search engine listing. If possible it should also contain some of your keywords in capitals.

Rule 3: Replace the text string in the first Content= above with your own short description of 20 to 25 words (around 150 characters including spaces), and including your most important keywords. Use capitals. Do this separately for each page on your Web site to reflect the page content.

Rule 4: Replace the text string in the second Content= above with your full list of up to 200 keywords, without allowing any word (even if it is in various phrases) to occur more often than three times. Do this separately for each page on your Web site to reflect the page content.

Rule 5: Try to ensure that the keywords for your page appear several times in the text on the page, particularly near the top. Don't just put a list of them at the end on their own, and don't make the text too stilted to weave them in.

Rule 6: Make sure that every page has a link back to your home page, and that there are plain (non-graphic) links from your home page to each of the other pages, even if you need some small links at the bottom of the page and you go through several pages to get from your home to the others.

Rule 7: Re-do this whole job at least every six months.

Robots also collect their data by using scanners and looking through newsgroups or USENET postings, including published mailing lists, archives, etc. As you can imagine, these links then "snowball" into other links and before you know it the robot is overloading the network and servers. In the early days there were occasions when robots visited WWW servers and created havoc, swamping servers with rapid-fire requests, or retrieving the same files repeatedly, to mention but two of the problems they created. These deficiencies have since been put right and many annoying faults ironed out. Furthermore, a useful standard has also been created for the exclusion of robots from particularly sensitive areas on servers. The standard was established in 1993-1994 and helps to indicate to robots which parts of the server they are working on should not be accessed.[8]

Once the robot has accessed the site, how does it decide what to index or put into its database?

> If an indexing robot knows about a document, it may decide to analyse it and insert it into its database. How this is done depends on the robot: some robots index the HTML Titles, or the first few paragraphs, or parse the entire HTML file and index all words, with weightings depending on HTML constructs, etc. Some look at the META tag, which is found in the header of the HTML document along with other special hidden tags.[9]

At the top of an HTML document there is coded information that a robot can automatically find because it looks for certain character strings such as META or TITLE, etc., and the data that follow the tag helps the robot to index useful information. More sophisticated robots look at the entire HTML document, index all the words, and even put a weighting on the most frequently used words.

There are essentially two types of robots: general ones like Lycos, Web Crawler, Infoseek, etc., and subject specific robots such as Peregrinator (an index of mathematics and statistics). Both types of robots are included in an annotated listing.[10] This site claims that these engines can search the Net automatically and that some of them can even learn information preferences. Once they have been 'taught' the preferences they can continue any mundane and repetitive tasks of searching, updating or modifying information. These products are not free, so for purposes of this article I have not investigated them. Nevertheless, the listing is a useful site to visit and provides a good starting place for examining supplementary programmes.

Another helpful listing[11] is simply an alphabetical listing of both general and subject specific robots. The links do not go directly to the robot site, but show details relating to the robot, such as owner, e-mail address, URL, and a brief description of the robot, and much more. This site includes information on robots ranging from AltaVista's Scooter (the robot which runs the huge AltaVista search engine) to Cassandra, developed as part of an MSc at the Moscow Institute of Physics and Technology. If you want to look at a small user-friendly robot, have a look at MOMspider (Multi-owner Maintenance Spider).[12]

A great deal more could be said about robots, and in places I have intentionally not filled in further detail in order to whet your appetite. The best site for all robots and intelligent agents is Botspot,[13] where there is a wealth of up-to-date information. This site is frequently referred to by other sites on related subjects. Incidentally, the Bookstore section of Botspot is linked to Amazon which is an excellent on-line US bookseller.

Search Engines

A search engine is a program that searches through data, usually of some similar format. In the context of the Web, the search engines search through databases of HTML documents gathered by a robot. As library and information professionals, we have been using search engines since on-line searching began. The difference with Web search engines is their symbiosis with robots and the scale of the data that they collect and retrieve, through examining indexes of HTML documents.

Let us look at an example of how a Web search engine was built. One of the most successful and useful search engines is AltaVista.[14] This URL will take you to the main AltaVista site. It all began in the spring of 1995, when a researcher from Digital's Western Research Lab, Louis Monier, was having lunch. What emerged was the robot Scooter and a full text index of the entire Internet. This was brought about by a phenomenal amount of hardware and committed Digital research staff. It was very much a matter of the right people in the right place at the right time: no start-up company could afford the research staff and no university could afford the equipment. By August 1995 research had progressed so that:

> one index would hold every word for the entire Web. Scooter could fetch pages at a rate more than a hundred times faster than anything then available. The full-text indexing software could

index these pages as fast as Scooter could fetch them and provide a complete representation of all the text on the Web. It could very quickly handle queries that included phrases, complex combinations of terms and unique structural elements of Web and newsgroup articles, and it would rank matches so pages that were most likely to be useful would appear at the top of the list.[15]

As you can see there is a clear relationship between the robot and the search engine, and these two components together allow you to search the Web.

Different Types of Search Engines

AltaVista is not the only search engine available which uses a robot to gather the HTML documents. "It is reassuring to know that there are only eight search engines that cover a significant part of the Internet,"[16] says Richard E. Peterson, Professor of Financial Economics and Institutions at the University of Hawaii. They are AltaVista, Excite, Hot Bot, Info Seek, Lycos, Open Text, Ultra, and Web Crawler. Each one falls into the category of robot generated WWW indexes, and it is important that you have a look at each one, since each offers something different.

There are many articles available in the computer press and also in librarianship journals which analyse output from particular searches across all these search engines.[17] Several factors determine the success of this type of search engine. Chief among them are size, content, currency of the database, speed of searching, availability of search features, the design and ease of use of the interface, and how the robot is programmed to gather the data. An excellent paper outlining the features and strengths and weakness of Web search engines is Jian Liu.[18] The most useful aspect of this paper is the way it relates search features to an individual search engine. For example, it tells you that AltaVista has simple and advanced queries, phrase searching in quotes, truncation with a *, required word/phrase (+), fielded searches on "link" "title" and URL, and a "near" operator which works within 10 words, and that three output formats are available. Liu does the same detailed analysis for Hot Bot, Info Seek, Excite Search, Web Crawler, Lycos, and Open Text, set out as bullet points for easy reference.

In addition to the robot type search engines there are also directories.[19] These are large searchable lists of Web pages or other Internet resources, usually organised into subject categories or alphabetical lists. The creators of these directories gather their information, and people enter it into the search engine's database. Generally they have smaller databases than the robot type (tens of thousands of pages of HTML rather than millions), but they can be more discriminating, for they include only those resources which are judged to be of value. Some notable ones are Yahoo, Magellan, Excite, and Deja News.

Another type of useful search engine currently available is the Meta search engine, such as Configurable Unified Search Interface (CUSI) and Simultaneous Unified Search Index (SUSI). CUSI[20] permits the checking of related resources without having to navigate and re-type the keywords and is a good listing of other search sources. The service divides into seven separate sections each with a pair of search boxes. Categories include WWW Indexes, robot-generated WWW Indexes, other Internet Indexes, software, people, documents, and dictionaries. The user enters the search term into any one of the seven search boxes and then chooses the required search engine by selecting the service in the next box to the right. Below each set of search boxes is an anno-tated listing describing all the search engines available in that catego-ry. It is possible to search any of the services listed either within CUSI using the search boxes or outside CUSI by clicking on the annotated link.

SUSI provides simultaneous searching of multiple Internet search engines and integrates the complete set of results. It has the advantage of a single location and common user interface for querying many diverse databases. The search tool is called Savvy Search[21] and in-cludes choices of keyword, sources (such as WWW, news, software, etc.) and gives various options like how many documents to display, what format, and whether to integrate the results or list them separate-ly for each search engine.

There is no shortage of information available on the Internet, and that is one of its problems. There is a comprehensive review[22] which looks at search services throughout the Internet, establishes a typology, examines strengths and weaknesses, and explores development trends.

Listings of Search Engines

There are many useful listings of search engines and search sources. Some contain simple links to the search sites such as Internet Magazine's list[23] of 50 quality search tools. Others, such as Virtual Search Engines,[24] include search boxes so you don't have to go directly to the search site.

Choosing a Search Engine

Having examined a few types and listings, you may still be baffled as to which search engine to choose for your particular query. It depends on how you want to search. Everything contained in a search engine is a mystery until you start to use it. The enquiry box is blank until you start entering different keywords, refining your searches, and trying again and again. Even when you have tried several times, you cannot be sure you have a complete picture of what the database contains. What you do have is a series of search results that emerge from various keywords you have entered, provided by automatic indexes and gathered by automatic robots.

Alternatively, if you wish to browse or surf the Internet, then the hierarchical arrangement of directories with their categories and sub-categories–created by people, not automatically trawled by robots–provides quite a different picture than a blank search box. In this sense, the Internet is like a book: search engines provide the index and directories are the table of contents. Both have their merits and it is a boon that there is the choice.

If the query is specific and the keywords are precise and have few synonyms, then do an index search. Use AltaVista, which is recognised to be the largest and the best, with Hot Bot close behind. On the other hand, if you want to browse and your query is of broad, general interest, then directories such as Yahoo will suit your purpose. The greatest difficulty is being comprehensive, because there is just so much information. When you need that sort of coverage, try everything, but start with SUSI.

A point of interest regarding search engines and directories is that in one instance they too are symbiotic. Firstly, Yahoo's listings are hierarchical and produced by people, but when you search you are using AltaVista's robot-based automatic search software. That makes Yahoo into an extraordinary Web searching tool: it has a hierarchical category structure but it also uses one of the largest databases and fastest search engines available. This makes a very powerful combination.

If you would like to choose for yourself, look at Search Engine Watch.[25] This site welcomes "researchers, librarians and general web surfers who want to know how to find things better using search engines." This impressive site provides review charts, statistics, monthly comparisons, trend analyses, and audience research of all the major search engines.

Getting the Most from Your Search

Browsing the Internet is so easy that no one needs to teach it: that's the beauty of it. The notion of surfing was first coined in 1994 by Jean Armour Polly who recorded that she

> wanted something that expressed the fun I had using the Internet, as well as hit on the skill, and yes endurance necessary to use it well. I also needed something that could evoke a sense of randomness, chaos, and even danger. I wanted something fishy, net-like, nautical. At the time I was using a mousepad from the Apple Library in Cupertino, California, famous for inventing and appropriating pithy sayings and printing them on sportswear and mousepads. The one I had, pictured a surfer on a big wave. 'Information Surfer' it said. 'Eureka,' I said and had my metaphor.[26]

Browsing hierarchical or alphabetical listings is pretty straightforward. Getting down to the mysterious business of using search engines and key words is much more complex.

Here are a few hints and tips.

- It is better to do many narrow searches than to make your search too broad.
- When possible use "AND" or "PHRASE"–otherwise most search engines assume an "OR" search.
- Use the best search engine first, because if you are just looking to browse then one search is probably sufficient. However, if you are seeking comprehensive coverage, try everything but start with a meta search engine. Another reason for using multiple search engines is that the ranking should return the best matches first, and the indexing done by different engines can be quite different, returning different results with different engines.
- Where possible, use subject specific search engines.
- Enter your keywords entirely in lower case, as some engines are case sensitive.
- Put the most important word first, as some search engines can also be sensitive to word order.

- Use the exact phrase option if looking for a name or something very specific.
- Use bookmarks when you find useful sites. This practice can save a lot of time. Bookmarks are available on both major browsers. They store URLs for future use. In addition it is possible to structure numerous bookmarks by adding subject categories using "folders." This creates a more organised hierarchical arrangement of your bookmarks.

Some limitations to watch out for.

- If timeliness is important, check when the site was last updated.
- Be aware that most of the information on the Web is American, so watch spellings of words such as programme, humour, colour.
- When you get a '404 Error' don't panic–it simply means the page is no longer available at that URL.
- Look at the URL and try going up the tree to the home page. Simply shorten the URL to the first / section, which will usually be that of the home page; the rest of the pathname identifies other pages at the site. For example, the URL for http://www.ouc.bc.ca/libr/connect96/search.htm has a first / section www.ouc.bc.ca.

In addition, the WWW provides a generous sampling of tutorials. A recommended few include:

- Tonic,[27] which is a good overview of the Internet and is UK based. Though it is a little out of date, many of the principles it presents are still sound and it is quite fun.
- At the Internet Training Zone[28] some of the URLs are no longer available, but on the whole it provides a lot of useful information. It also is UK based.
- If you are just starting to search and want to develop some good habits, the Library of the University of California at Berkeley[29] provides an excellent tutorial, extensive and well worth the time. I particularly like the way they go through a search strategy in cycles, explaining the first search, second search, etc. The template they provide is a useful reference for any search, and they include sample searches and links to useful sources.
- An example of a specific subject tutorial is one that is for lawyers.[30] It demonstrates how to find answers to some sample legal questions.

The Responsibility of the Web Master

Effective searching rests not only with the search engines, directories and robots, but also in creating Web pages which acknowledge these tools and assist them in analysing and retrieving the information contained in the HTML code. I mentioned earlier the seven rules for search engine registration.[31] This is a good checklist on how to go about registering your site with the main search engines. If you are considering Web authoring or have created Web pages, then look at Advanced Web Marketing.[32] This is another good checklist that will help you to disseminate your work so more people can use it, and isn't that the point of creating a page? Lastly, there exists an all-purpose general WWW Information Pack.[33] This useful site helps you to use the Web, author for the Web, and master the more advanced topics such as Java and ActiveX.

CONCLUSION

This paper has provided an overview of the Internet, WWW, robots, search engines, and Web mastering, in an effort to show how they work and what they can do for you. It is hoped that the reader will now have some understanding of how the Internet came about, how robots work, and which search engines are best suited for particular types of queries. It is possible to improve retrieval by following a few rules when creating Web pages. The Internet is here to stay. It has had considerable impact even in its short life. The greatest reference tool of the 20th Century is ripe for exploitation, and armed with a little knowledge of how things work, the information profession is in a unique position to utilise and exploit it.

NOTES

1. Gwyneth Tseng, Alan Poulter, Debra Hiom, *The Library and Information Professional's Guide to the Internet* (London: Library Association Publishing, 1997).
2. Catherine Hume, "Book Review," *ITs News* December 36 (1997): 42-43.
3. Rich Schwerin, "Explorer vs. Navigator"
<URL: http://www.znet.com/pccomp/features/fea096/sub1.html> (1996) Seen 28 July 1998.
4. "What is a Bot?: The Spot for all Bots & Intelligent Agents"
<URL: http:// botspot.com/what-is-a-bot/html> (1998) Seen 9 June 1998.

5. "The Web Robots FAQ"
<URL: http://info.webcrawler.com/mak/projects/robots/faq.html> Seen 24 November 1999.

6. As 5. p. 4.

7. "Actinics seven rules for search engine registration"
<URL: http://www.actinic.co.uk/index.htm> (25 March 1998) Seen 24 November 1999.

8. "A Standard for Robot Exclusion"
<URL: http://info.webcrawler.com/mak/projects/robots/norobots.html> (30 June 1994) Seen 24 November 1999.

9. As 5. p. 4.

10. "Bots, Agents & Spiders"
<URL: http://www.yorku.ca/admin/cst/e2ngines/bots.htm> Seen 28 July 1998.

11. "Database of Web Robots, Overview of Raw files"
<URL: http://info.webcrawler.com/mak/projects/robots/active/html/raw.html> Seen 24 November 1999.

12. Ray Fielding "MOMspider: Multi-owner Maintenance Spider"
<URL: http:// www.ics.uci.edu/pub/websoft/MOMspider/> (13 May 1998) Seen 24 November 1999.

13. "Bot Spot: Site Map: The Spot for all Bots and Intelligent Agents"
<URL: http://botspot.com/site_map/> (1998) Seen 28 July 1998.

14. "AltaVista home page"
<URL: http://www.altavista.digital.com> (1995- 1998) Seen 24 November 1999.

15. "About AltaVista"
<URL: http://mnetsearch.metronet.co.uk/av/content/about_our_story_2.htm> Seen 11 June 1998.

16. Richard E. Peterson, "Harvesting Information from the Internet Using Search Engines"
<URL: http://www2.hawaii.edu/~rpeterso/harvest2.htm> (March 1997) Seen 24 November 1999.

17. John Scott Cree and Ron Le Bruin "The search for the best engine" *Library Association Record-Library Technology Supplement* 3:3 (June 1998): 45-47.

18. Jian Liu, "Understanding WWW Search Tools"
<URL: http://www.indiana.edu/~librcsd/search/old/> (September 1996) Seen 24 November 1999.

19. "How can I find information on the Web?"
<URL: http://www.novtech.co.uk/chap4.html> (1998) Seen 24 November 1999.

20. Nexor "CUSI"
<URL: http://www.nexor.com/public/cusi/cusi.html> (1995) Seen 13 July 1998.

21. Daniel Dreilinger, "Savvy Search"
<URL: http://www.cs.colostate.edu/~dreiling/smartform.html> (1995-1998) Seen 28 July 1998.

22. T. Koch, A. Ardo, A. Brummer and S. Lundberg, "The building and maintenance of robot based internet search services: A review of current indexing and data collection methods"

<URL: http://www.ub21u.se:80/desire/radar/reports/D3.11/> (1996) Seen 25 July 1998.

23. "Search engines"
<URL: http://www.internet-magazine.com/resources/search.htm> Seen 28 July 1998.

24. "Virtual Search Engines–Plus Over 1,000 fully functional search engines with 50 Categories"
<URL: http://www.dreamscape.com/frankvad/search.html> (1998) Seen 24 Novenber 1999.

25. Danny Sullivan, "Welcome to Search Engine Watch"
<URL: http://searchenginewatch.com/> (1998) Seen 24 July 1998.

26. As 16. p. 5.

27. "TONIC"
<URL: http://www.netskills.ac.uk/TONIC/> (1997) Seen 24 November 1999.

28. "The Internet Training Zone"
<URL: http://www.haste.demon.co.uk/bi-intor.htm> Seen 11 June 1998.

29. Teaching Library Internet Workshops, University of California, "Finding Information on the Internet: A TUTORIAL"
<URL: http://www.lib.berkeley.edu/teachinglib/guides/internet/findinfo.html> (30 June, 1998) Seen 24 November 1999.

30. "Web Surfing Workshop for Lawyers; Search Exercise"
<URL: http://www.law.ed.ac.uk/ws-srch.htm> Seen 11 June 1998.

31. As 7. p. 2.

32. Advanced Web Marketing, "Web Marketing FAQ"
<URL: http://fenet.co.uk/awm/awm100.htm> Seen 24 November 1999.

33. Novotech, "WWW Information Pack"
<URL: http://www.novtech.co.uk/index.html> (1998) Seen 24 November 1999.

Internet Search Engines:
Understanding Their Design
to Improve Information Retrieval

Kurt I. Munson

SUMMARY. The relationship between the methods currently used for indexing the World Wide Web and the programs, languages, and protocols on which the World Wide Web is based is examined. Two methods for indexing the Web are described, directories being briefly discussed while search engines are considered in detail. The automated approach used to create these tools is examined with special emphasis on the parts of a document used in indexing. Shortcomings of the approach are described. Suggestions for effective use of Web search engines are given. *[Article copies available for a fee from The Haworth Document Delivery Service: 1-800-342-9678. E-mail address: getinfo@haworthpressinc.com <Website: http://www.haworthpressinc.com>]*

KEYWORDS. World Wide Web, indexing, search engines, robots, Internet

The tools used to locate information on the World Wide Web are both similar to and different from library catalogs and indexes. Library-based cataloging and indexing rely heavily upon human in-

---

Kurt I. Munson is Head of Client Services, Galter Health Sciences Library, Northwestern University, 303 East Chicago Avenue, Chicago, IL 60611 (kmunson@nwu.edu).

[Haworth co-indexing entry note]: "Internet Search Engines: Understanding Their Design to Improve Information Retrieval." Munson, Kurt I. Co-published simultaneously in *Journal of Internet Cataloging* (The Haworth Information Press, an imprint of The Haworth Press, Inc.) Vol. 2, No. 3/4, 2000, pp. 47-60; and: *Internet Searching and Indexing: The Subject Approach* (ed: Alan R. Thomas, and James R. Shearer) The Haworth Information Press, an imprint of The Haworth Press, Inc., 2000, pp. 47-60. Single or multiple copies of this article are available for a fee from The Haworth Document Delivery Service [1-800-342-9678, 9:00 a.m. - 5:00 p.m. (EST). E-mail address: getinfo@haworthpressinc.com].

47

volvement. In contrast, Web indexing is automated. This fundamental difference requires the user to address Web indexes differently from library catalogs. To find material effectively on the Web, a searcher needs to know how Web finding guides are created, what they are designed to do, and how to use them to find resources.

RELATIONSHIP BETWEEN WEB INDEXES AND THE PROGRAMS AND LANGUAGES ON WHICH THE WEB IS BASED

Web indexes do not stand alone as traditional indexes do. Rather, Web indexes have a symbiotic relationship with the contents of the Web. These indexes are created by and accessed by using the *hypertext, languages, protocols,* and transfer mechanics of the Web. "The WWW [sic] project was originally developed to provide a *distributed hypermedia system* which one could easily access–from any desktop computer–and spread information across the world."[1] Web indexes are a product of the distributed hypermedia technology upon which they and the things to which they provide access are based. As a result, a searcher cannot understand Web search engines without a basic knowledge of the underlying structure and building blocks of the Web and by extension the search engines.

When users call up a Web page, they type a *URL* (Uniform Resource Locator), into a program called a *browser*. The URL is the Internet address for the Web page. A browser is a software program on the user's machine that communicates with a *document server*, the machine on which the page is stored. The browser then retrieves the pages and displays them. Browsers use a protocol called *HTTP* (Hypertext Transfer Protocol) developed in 1989, to contact a remote machine on the Internet and request that a copy of a page be sent to the machine that has the browser loaded on it. The page is written in *HTML* (Hypertext Markup Language) which the Web browser is designed to read.

The HTML file contains the text, images, and sound that the user sees. It also contains formatting codes, embedded hypertext links that call other Web pages, and additional coding to define how the page is displayed on the monitor. HTML is a simple yet powerful language. It has three primary strengths. First, it is platform independent, so it does not require a specific operating system. A HTML page can thus be read by any machine with the appropriate software. Second, HTML pages can include graphics, moving images, and sounds. Third, HTML allows for words or images in the page to serve as links to other pages. The 1993 introduction of Mosaic, the first Web browser with the ability to display graphics and color, led to a massive increase in Web-based resources.

The coalescence of HTTP, HTML, and graphical Web browsers led to the explosive growth of the Web. By 1994, the Web had grown to a point where it was no longer possible to keep track of all existing Web sites. Computer scientists and their students began to create tools to index and provide access to the ever increasing number of sites. Two types of finding guides developed–lists and indexes. These tools use different methods to generate their guides. Recently, hybrids like Lycos TOP 5% have come into being.

These two types of finding guides for the Internet take alternative approaches to organizing the pages to which they are linked. Lists, as a matter of policy, focus on classification of a smaller set of pages. For lists, people analyze the pages so that they can place the pages within the hierarchy of a directory, so grouping like pages together. Search engines build indexes using an automated approach devoid of human intervention that relies upon the words in the page to provide access points. The search engines focus on developing very large indexes hoping to cover the entire Web.

The lists developed into *directories*, like Yahoo (http://www.yahoo.com). Resources of this type have many similar characteristics to more traditional library indexes and are therefore only briefly described. Directories seek to collocate Internet pages using a classificatory scheme much like the Dewey Decimal system. The use of a classificatory scheme makes this type of Web index quite familiar as it is akin to the system used in libraries. This method of indexing is also similar to traditional library indexing in that human indexers select the subdivision where the resource is placed. Yahoo also relies upon recommendations submitted by users for additional pages to be included in the directory. This system allows users to browse through a variety of sources on like topics by selecting a subject and its subdivisions, as in the case of a user wanting a list of all the colleges and universities in Chicago, Illinois. Yahoo, as the largest directory, is a good place to start.

Directories are also useful if a user knows of one page and would like to find similar ones. The user can run a search for the known item and then check the categories where that page is located. A searcher who knows about a Web site on Medieval History called Netserf and wants to find other Medieval Studies Web sites can enter the name of the page into the search box.[2] The system will display the categories, Arts: Art History: Periods and Movements: Medieval Art, Arts: Humanities: History: Middle Ages: Indices, Arts: Humanities: Literature: Periods and Movements: Medieval, so that the searcher can locate where additional pages are listed in the directory.

The indexes developed into *search engines*. This type of Web indexing is very different from library indexing. It does not rely upon human indexers because computers do the indexing. This fully automated process results in an index with very different characteristics from a traditional index and is described below in greater detail.

A search engine is "software that *parses* a user query, compares it to an index, retrieves documents that the index indicates match the user query, and returns a set of results."[3] The process begins with the user entering the search terms, for example, German Shepherd. The search engine software then parses or analyzes the statement so that it can be broken down into units which are converted into machine language. The software then looks for matching records in the index, selects out those matching records, and displays them as search results. Search engines rely upon the user's choice of search terms to generate a hit list. Some examples of search engines are AltaVista (http://www.altavista.digital.com), Lycos (http://www.lycos.com), Excite (http://www.excite.com), and HotBot (http://www.hotbot.com). These are the search engines used in examples below.

CREATION OF SEARCH ENGINES

In 1993, computer scientists drew upon computerized database design to develop their Web search engines. Thus computerized databases design–not library indexing–underlies all search engines. In databases, the blocks from which everything else is constructed are characters, letters, numbers, and all other symbols. A group of characters makes up a field, collections of fields make up records, and groups of records make up databases.

A search engine system is composed of three parts. First, it must have some tool that can generate a list of new sites and examine known sites. Second, it needs a database of page abstracts that describe the sites. Third, it requires a search program with a user interface that can run searches against the database. Each of these three parts is examined in greater detail below.

Generation of a Site List

The tool that Web indexes use to generate a list of new sites and examine known sites is called a *robot* which is "a program that automatically traverses the Web's hypertext structure by retrieving a document, and recursively retrieving all documents that are referenced."[4] Robots are also known as spiders, Web crawlers, and worms. All of these programs work like a person using a browser to surf the Web. The process is illustrated in Figure 1.

First, the robot makes a list of all the links from some starting page, page #1 to other pages: link *A*, link *B*, link *C*. Second, it examines all the links, *A*, *B*, and *C*, to insure that they are live and lead to other pages. Then, it follows a link, *A*, to page #2 and examines page #2's links. The robot repeats the process until it reaches a page with no links or a dead link, like page #3 in the figure, it moves back one level

FIGURE 1. The Process by Which Robots Locate Additional Web Resources

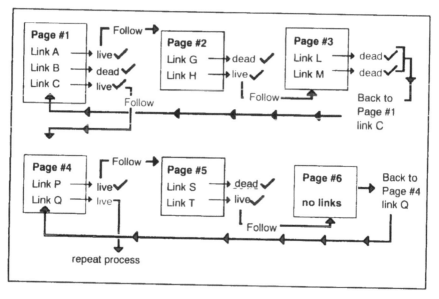

and proceeds to the next live link: page #1 link C in the figure. The robot repeats the entire process over and over gradually working its way across the Web. Simply put, "a web robot is a browser with an autopilot."[5]

Robots can be used for a variety of jobs: indexing, validating HTML codes, and gathering statistics. Indexing robots visit pages with the specific purpose of creating an abstract of that page's content and adding the information about it to a data set. The robot then examines all of the links from that page to other pages. Working through each link, the robot repeats the process of visiting pages linked to the original page and adding the information about those pages to the data set.

The size and constant state of flux of the Web makes robot-based indexing necessary. There are now over 9,169,898 *domains*,[6] or machine addresses like www.galter.nwu.edu, registered with countless pages on them. Web sites move between servers, change addresses, and frequently disappear entirely. *Link rot*, the problem of hypertext links that point to invalid addresses, is also a problem. In the words of Martijn Kostor,[7] "where humans cannot cope with the amount of information it is attractive to let the computer do the work." Unfortunately, robots view all links as equal. Indexing robots will index all the pages on a site unless they are told what to exclude. To this end the *Robot Exclusion Standard* was created. This standard defines a file, *robots.txt*, that tells a robot examining a site what to ignore. The system administrator or Webmaster composes a file of plain text, names it robots.txt, and places this file in the Web site's main directory. This file informs the robots what directories, pages, and resources on that Web site should not be examined and therefore not indexed. Increased use of the robot exclusion standard will reduce the number of ephemeral pages indexed in the search engines.

Database of Page Abstracts

The contents of the page abstracts that the robots generate provide the building blocks for the database. The companies that provide Web indexes use proprietary algorithms to generate their indexing databases. As a result, the user cannot easily determine what data is collected by the robot to build the index. AltaVista and Lycos provide a glimpse into what information is collected and then indexed. AltaVista's robot "scooter" examines "all the HTML information on a page:

all text, ALT text for images, links (hrefs and images), anchors, title, description and keyword META tags, applet and ActiveX object names, the page's URL, its host name (www.foo.com) and its domain name (com)."[8] Simply put, for AltaVista the words in the page, the hypertext links, images, and address information are indexed. Lycos in contrast indexes the words in the page's title, headings and subheadings, all the words in the first 20 lines, and the 100 most weighty words derived by an algorithm that ranks word placement and frequency. These examples show the substantial number of elements which might be part of a Web page and which the search engine robots examine and add selectively to their databases.

Unfortunately, most producers of Web indexes are not forthcoming in explaining what parts of a Web page they examine to create the page abstracts that make up the contents of their databases. Index producers occasionally explain what they exclude from indexing. For example, Excite excludes metadata.[9] Metadata, identified by special HTML tags, records additional information about a page. Metadata tags describe three aspects of a Web page: the content of the page, the owner of the intellectual property, and the instantiation of the page. Contents metadata allows an author to describe the page's subject content, coverage and relation to other sources. The intellectual property tags define the creator, publisher, and contributors. The instantiation tags tell when the page was created or updated, its type, format, and its URL. The metadata tag for subject keywords, especially those using controlled vocabulary, is especially helpful for searching.

SEARCH PROGRAM

The third part of the search engine is the search screen. This is where users input their searches. It is also where any search refinements are made.

Search engines are commercial enterprises. Unlike traditional library indexes, like those produced by the H. W. Wilson company and others, the search engines do not rely upon subscriptions to generate their profits. Rather, advertising provides their chief source of revenue. Since the search engines are in competition with each other they tend to "provide simpler interfaces with fewer advanced retrieval functions. Sometimes advanced functions and even help information seems to be hidden. The interfaces are crowded by additional entertaining facilities and advertisements which sometimes make it difficult to find the search service itself."[10] The user interface is the only part of the index that the user sees and therefore is the place where the advertising is visible.

While the size and changing nature of the Web make robot-based indexing attractive, a number of problems exist with the robot-generated method of indexing. First, robots view the Web as flat. Being robots, they cannot evaluate Web pages: all Web pages are equal to them. Second, the robots cannot correct for low quality Web pages. If the author of the page does not include or does not code the page's HTML correctly, the quality of the record created by the robot will suffer. Robots cannot correct misspelled words or index missing HTML codes. Third, the robots can only locate Web pages linked to ones they have already located. Given that the robots follow hypertext links to locate materials, if other Web pages do not link to a page that page will not be indexed. Fourth, the robot exclusion standard is not widely followed. "Many information providers forget to exclude general robots from indexing documents of entirely personal, local or short-time interest, respectively low-quality documents. Those documents are in great numbers encumbering the search databases and deteriorating most search results."[10] The robots simply examine what is there, relying entirely upon the words of the page being indexed.

EFFECTIVE SEARCHING

The nature and makeup of the Web coupled with the information extracted from Web pages produce indexes which are unlike library catalogs. A search in a Web index is a search against the "fields" that describe the Web page in the database. Running a search in these indexes is a matter of selecting the right type of index, i.e., a search engine or a directory and using the available tools to produce as relevant a search as possible.

As with traditional library-based resources, selecting the right tool is the first step to finding the desired information. Is the user trying to develop an extensive list of Web pages on a topic? Is the search for the location of a known item? Is the search for a unique item? The searcher's information needs will determine what type of Web page to use.

Finding the best or highest quality topical resource using the Web can be difficult since the robots that generate the search engines lack the ability to evaluate pages for content. The search engine producers recognize this and have begun to hybridize their services by adding small highly selective directories to their services that provide access to the better sites. For example, Lycos provides a service called Lycos Top 5%. According to its home page,[11] "TOP 5% is a selective directory of top-shelf sites rated by the Web's most experienced reviewers."

The companies that produce Web search engines place stronger emphasis on methods of tweaking the search strategy than on refining the information in the databases. As a result, search engines provide a number of tools for defining and refining a search. Unfortunately, users initially see the basic search screens but these screens do not provide access to the majority of the tools for refining and narrowing a search. If users wish to do more complicated or clearly defined searches, they should select the advanced search screens and they must learn how to use them effectively.

Searchers must keep in mind that each search engine has a different syntax for running searches. Also, the different search engines provide different methods for refining a search. The user cannot assume that a search option that works in one search engine will work in another. Reading the help screens is a critical part of using these tools effectively. The help pages provided for Webmasters, the people who design and maintain both Web pages and Web sites, are also a source of information for searchers. These pages provide Webmasters with instructions on how to compose pages, which HTML tags to use, and how to organize a page to maximize its retrieval during a search. These pages can inform the searcher on which parts of the Web page are examined and abstracted in the indexing process.

It is important to understand the search engines' definition of a word: a word for a search engine can be any string of characters such as a real word like history or a URL like www.healthweb.org. Blank spaces and characters that have special meanings in URLs are interpreted by the databases as separating words. For example, a "/" is interpreted as defining a directory, "%" is used in search strings.

All search engines use relevancy ranking systems to sort the search results. These systems work by examining the location of a word within the page, the frequency with which the word occurs in the page, and the length of the page. For example, HotBot ranks pages according to the number of times a word occurs in the page, if the word is in the page's title, if the word is listed in the keyword meta tag, and the length of the page.[12] Lycos allows the searcher to adjust the relative importance of each of the search words within the page. For example, the searcher can require the word be in the title, near the beginning of the text, or frequently throughout the text. The word's location within the page can be weighted along with the word's occurrence within the title tag field. By fine tuning the relevancy ranking system, a searcher can adjust the position of a page in the list of search results. The user accesses these options on the Lycos Pro Advanced[13] search screen. Relevancy ranking systems place shorter pages with a specified word in the title, metadata, and frequently throughout the text earlier in the output list.

Boolean logic provides additional methods for refining a search. AND, OR, and NOT are used in most search engines. A searcher can nest search terms by using parentheses to build an in-depth search. In addition to Boolean logic, search engines frequently use plus (+) and minus (−) signs to indicate if a word must be included in or excluded from a search. A searcher can also define relationships between words using adjacency operators. For example, in Lycos ADJ allows a user to find words adjacent to each other, NEAR within 25 words of each other, and BEFORE one word before the other.[14] These operators can be refined by specifying distance between the words. For example, Bergen NEAR/5 Norway will retrieve pages where the city of Bergen's name occurs within five words of the country name Norway.

Some search engines provide tools for truncation or wild cards. The asterisk (*) is the most common symbol for truncation and wild cards. In AltaVista, the asterisk can be used either at the end of a word or internally. To find the word "children" or "childhood," in AltaVista, the user would type child* into the search box. A search for women or woman would be entered as wom*n. Truncation and wild cards can be combined in AltaVista so the searcher could locate materials on men's or manhood by entering m*n*. Truncation should be used with caution. The "men's or manhood" example would also retrieve pages with the words manicure, mondial, munching, munson, etc.

Phrase searching should be used in Web search engines whenever possible because this reduces the number of problems with lexical ambiguity. AltaVista, Lycos, and Excite all provide for phrase searching by enclosing the phrase in quotation marks. Ambiguity creeps in when a word has multiple meanings. For example, the word "tree" can mean many things: a woody perennial plant, a directory structure in computer science, a listing of ancestors as in a family tree. Phrase searching allows the user to place the word in context and reduce the number of irrelevant hits. For example, a search for the genealogical software package "Family Tree Maker" would produce a relevant hit list on this software as opposed to a hit list of pages that discuss individual family histories.

In refining a search, problems frequently arise when a word has multiple meanings and adding additional words will not clarify the search. Unlike the subject headings fields in traditional library catalogs, Web pages do not contain fields for defining the subject content of a Web page. An alternate tool for conducting this type of search on the Web is needed. Boolean logic can be used, but the search frequently becomes a single word with a long string of other words to be excluded with a NOT operator. For example, a search for the Vikings would produce information on the Minnesota Vikings football team, the Viking space probe, and a sewing machine company. A user seeking information on the Vikings as the early medieval peoples of Scandinavia would thus retrieve much irrelevant material. AltaVista provides the ability to limit this search to pages that define the word Viking only in the desired context. The related searches option produces a list of pages where the search term is placed in context with other words. In the example above, the co-occurrence of the word Viking with other words like "norse, iceland, scandinavia, scandinavian, greenland, sagas, and icelandic is established by the retrieval algorithm."[15] Using pull down menus provided on the screen, the user selects a context for the search term by requiring or excluding a selection. This system affords the opportunity to limit a search as required.

Capitalization and case-sensitive searching can be used to limit a search. Search engines use varying degrees of case-sensitivity. Using all lower-case letters in a search will retrieve all records where those words are used. A search employing capitalization will retrieve only records with an exact match. A simple search in AltaVista for the capitalized words Oak Park[16] without any adjacency operators found 30,052 pages primarily about this Chicago suburb while the same search using lower case letters for the words oak park[17] found 32,236 pages. The same searches in HotBot resulted in 13,590 pages for "Oak Park"[18] and 15,050 pages for "oak park."[19] Case sensitive searching results in a slight reduction in pages with a slight improvement in relevancy. It is most effective when used in combination with other limits.

The lack of controlled vocabulary on the Web requires creative methods for limiting searches as seen above. The most effective is field searching, which is similar to doing a search for an author and a title in a library catalog. Different search engines allow for different types of field searching. Generally, a user can limit a search to titles, domains, URLs, and images. The methods for limiting are explained in greater detail below.

Lycos allows a user to limit a search to the title of a page. In a HTML page, the title is defined by the <Title> tag and is the text that appears above the browser's menu bar. It is not the initial words in the body of the page–these appear below the browser's menu bar. This method of searching assumes that the topic of the page will be stated in the title.

Using a domain name as part of a search provides another efficient way of limiting the number of sites retrieved. Domain names are standardized: .gov, .edu, .com, and .org for United States federal government sites, colleges and universities in the United States, commercial sites and organizations respectively. By combining a topical search with a likely domain name, a searcher can limit the search to a type of site that is most likely to have information on the topic. For example, if a user wanted a list of different American universities' guidelines for writing dissertations, that person could limit the search to sites with URLs ending in .edu, the ending which denotes colleges and universities.

Host names can also be used to limit a search. This method builds upon domain name searching by moving from a type of address to a specific computer, or host's, name. Using this method is roughly equivalent to searching by ZIP or postal code. For example, a search for government information on groundwater from the Environmental Protection Agency could be limited to just .gov domains since the Environmental Protection Agency is a government body. But by adding the Environmental Protection Agency's server's host name, www.epa.gov, the search is directed to look only on that server for groundwater information. An example search in HotBot, using the super search, combined the word groundwater in the search the Web field with the phrase .epa.gov in the location/domain box[20] produced information from the specified server only.

The nature of the Web, the type of information stored in the databases that the search engines use, and the total reliance on the part of the robots upon the page author's inclusion of text and codes produce search engines that are different than library catalogs. The automated nature of Web indexing coupled with the uneven nature of the quality of the text and HTML codes created by authors results in "dirty" databases. "The input into the search services varies a great deal. Often it is so poor that the search-results are seriously influenced in a negative way."[10] The goal of the search engine creators is to provide tools that can produce as highly relevant search sets as possible within the limitations imposed by the quality of the records for individual Web pages which are identified in the database. Consequently, effective use of search engines involves creating queries that take advantage of both the information stored in the page abstract and the tools available to refine and focus a search. This is a skilled task and that skill is one that it is vital for a modern information specialist to acquire and apply.

NOTES

1. Gregory Gromov, *History of the Internet and WWW*
<URL: http://www.internetvalley.com/intval.html> Seen 26 July 1999.
2. *Yahoo Search*
<URL: http://search.yahoo.com/bin/search?p=netserf> Seen 26 July 1999.
3. Susan Maze, David Moxley and Donna J. Smith, *Neal-Schuman Authoritative Guide to Web Search Engines* (New York: Neal-Schuman, 1997), p. 165.
4. *The Web Robot FAQ*
<URL: http://info.webcrawler.com/mak/projects/robots/faq.html> Seen 26 July 1999.
5. Crawling the Web: A guide to robots, spiders, and other shadowy denizens of the Web *PC Magazine* 15:13 (1996): 277.
6. *WWW.domainstats.com Your guide to Domain Name statistics*
<URL: http://www.domainstats.com/> Seen 26 July 1999.
7. Martijn Koster, *Robots in the Web: Threat or treat?*
<URL: http://info.webcrawler.com/mak/projects/robots/threat-or-treat.html> (April, 1995) Seen 26 July 1999.
8. *AltaVista Search: FAQ-Webmaster*
<URL:http://www.altavista.digital.com/av/content/ques_webmaster.htm> Seen 19 December 1998.
9. *Getting listed on Excite*
<URL: http://www.excite.com/Info/listing.html> Seen 19 December 1998.

10. T. Koch, A. Ardö, A. Brümmer and S. Lundberg, *The building and mainte-nance of robot based Internet search services: A review of current indexing and data collection methods*
<URL: http://www.ub2.lu.se/desire/radar/reports/D3.11/tot.html> (26 September 1996) Seen 26 July 1999.

11. *Lycos Top 5% Home*
<URL: http://point.lycos.com/categories/> Seen 26 July 1999.

12. *HotBot FAQ: Results, Scoring, and Ranking*
<URL: http://www.hotbot.com/help/faq/questions/question2.asp> Seen 19 December 1998.

13. *Lycos Home Page*
<URL: http://lycospro.lycos.com/lycospro-nojava.html> Seen 26 July 1999.

14. *Lycos Help Guide Boolean Expressions*
<URL: http://www.lycos.com/help/lycospro-help.html#boolean> Seen 26 July 1999.

15. *AltaVista: Vikings*
<URL: http://www.altavista.digital.com./cgi-bin/query?pg=c9&kl=XX&q=Vikings> Seen 26 July 1999.

16. AltaVista: Simple Query Oak Park
<URL: http://www.altavista.digital.com/cgi-bin/query?pg=q&kl=XX&q=%22Oak+Park%22> Seen 26 July 1999.

17. AltaVista: Simple Query oak park
<URL: http://altavista.digital.com/cgi-bin/query?pg=q&kl=XX&q=oak+park> Seen 26 July 1999.

18. HotBot results: "Oak Park"
<URL: http://www.hotbot.com/?MT=%22Oak+Park%22&_v=2&OPs=MDRTP> Seen 26 July 1999.

19. HotBot results: "oak park"
<URL: http://www.hotbot.com/?MT=%22oak+park%22&NOS=10&top=dh> Seen 26 July 1999.

20. *HotBot results: groundwater (+1)*
<URL: http://www.hotbot.com/?clickSrc=search&MT=groundwater&SM=MC&LG=any &AM0=MC&AT0=words&AW0=&AM1=MN&AT1=words&AW1=&savenummod=2& date=within&DV=0&DR=newer&DM=1&DD=1&DY=98&FS=&RG=.com&RD=DM &Domain=epa.gov&PS=A&PD=&DC=10&DE=2&SUBMIT=SEARCH&_v=2&OPs= MDRTP&RD =DM&date=within&NUMMOD=2 > Seen 26 July 1999.

Signposts
on the Information Superhighway:
Indexes and Access

Susan MacDougall

SUMMARY. Users of the Information Superhighway need signposts to find their way to appropriate, accurate and current information. Given the sheer quantity of information, intellectual indexing is more relevant than ever, complementing and augmenting automatic keyword indexing. Signposts come in various forms including browser bookmarks, local, on-site and remote lists, indexes and directories, temporary search engine results, and metadata. The considerable body of theory on vocabulary control for online database searching can be adapted to index construction for the Internet. At the same time, there are unresolved issues concerning information quality, indexing decisions, and standards. *[Article copies available for a fee from The Haworth Document Delivery Service: 1-800-342-9678. E-mail address: getinfo@haworthpressinc.com <Website: http:// www.haworthpressinc.com>]*

KEYWORDS. World Wide Web, Internet, information access, subject indexing, intellectual indexing, metadata, vocabulary control

WHY SIGNPOSTS?

People need help to navigate the overwhelming amount of information on the 'Information Superhighway.' The purpose of signposting is

Susan MacDougall is Editor, East Asian Library Resources Group of Australia (EALRGA) (susan.macdougall@alianet.alia.org.au).

[Haworth co-indexing entry note]: "Signposts on the Information Superhighway: Indexes and Access." MacDougall, Susan. Co-published simultaneously in *Journal of Internet Cataloging* (The Haworth Information Press, an imprint of The Haworth Press, Inc.) Vol. 2, No. 3/4, 2000, pp. 61-79; and: *Internet Searching and Indexing: The Subject Approach* (ed: Alan R. Thomas, and James R. Shearer) The Haworth Information Press, an imprint of The Haworth Press, Inc., 2000, pp. 61-79. Single or multiple copies of this article are available for a fee from The Haworth Document Delivery Service [1-800-342-9678, 9:00 a.m. - 5:00 p.m. (EST). E-mail address: getinfo@haworthpressinc.com].

to create access to World Wide Web materials. By 'signpost' is meant an index term plus a locator, which link to an information resource. Signposts can be readily created using keywords, or single content-bearing words taken directly from the text. However, keywords are not very efficient, particularly when there is a large volume of information, since they result in high volume recall and low precision: that is, too much irrelevant information to sift through to find what is wanted. A case can be made for the use of controlled vocabularies to improve searching and retrieval. Free-text, uncontrolled terms have the advantage of using the words in the text and requiring little intellectual effort, but the disadvantage of failing to resolve ambiguities and take into account synonyms.

ABOUT INDEXING

Indexing techniques and processes for print materials are being adapted to the Web. Traditionally, indexing encompasses a variety of activities, the most important of which is subject indexing. Subject indexing requires intellectual effort and arguably cannot be replaced by automation, hence the term 'intellectual indexing.' Indexing a document involves entering author, title, and source fields as well as indexing personal and corporate names, geographic locations, historical periods, and subjects, and, for online bibliographic database indexing, summarising the content in an abstract.

It is generally accepted that there is a common core of indexing theory. Library science itself is permeated with indexing concepts.[1] There are diverse techniques and skills for different kinds of indexing.[2] Indexing straddles traditional library science and publishing activities: book and serial indexers are largely self-taught and tend to come from a writing/editing background, while database and Internet indexers often have a librarianship/computing background.[3]

Subject indexing consists of two major stages: content analysis, followed by the application of appropriate terminology, the 'translation phase.'[4] In the past,[4] a false distinction has often been drawn between subject indexing, classification, and subject cataloguing: the intellectual activity involved in the analysis process is the same in all types of indexing.

The content analysis stage of subject indexing involves subject classification, that is, forming classes of objects on the basis of their subject matter. At the translation stage, sources for allocating index terms vary between subject heading lists, thesauri, and classification schemes, but for effective use, they have in common the need to apply the most specific indexing or subject cataloguing terms available to each item. The combined descriptive and subject indexing techniques involve particular learned skills using nominated international or national standards, or in-house guidelines. Specific and detailed techniques apply to indexing different formats, which encompass the following:

Formats
- Books (back of book indexing)
- Books (summarisation for database entry)
- Databases
- Documents (various) for database entry
- Film
- Internet pages
- Internet sites
- Manuscripts
- Maps
- Microforms
- Multimedia
- Music
- Newspapers
- Pictures
- Reference works
- Serials (individual issues/cumulations)
- Sound recordings
- Videotapes

As well as a knowledge of indexing techniques, many subject areas require specialist subject knowledge, including: Genealogy, or family history; Law; Mathematics; Medicine; and the sciences, including Astronomy, Physics, Chemistry. Book indexers tend to specialise in one or two subject areas of indexing. When they achieve a certain standard, they can apply for registration to a society of indexers. Cataloguers do not have specific cataloguing registration requirements for the work of cataloguing, although they are normally qualified as professional librarians.

The differences between the types of indexing are marked. It cannot be assumed that a cataloguer can automatically create or contribute to a good book index or an indexer, a good catalogue, because the techniques and skills are so different. The chief difference between book and other types of indexing is that books require a one-off customised, exhaustive index based mainly on the author's vocabulary, with the addition of entry terms and cross references. Most other indexing, particularly for bibliographic databases, requires the use of a continuing controlled vocabulary in the form of a thesaurus or subject heading list covering wide ranging topics. Cataloguing is a specialised form of indexing using the specific standards Anglo-American Cataloguing Rules, 2nd edition (AACR2)[5] and Library of Congress Subject Headings (LCSH).[6]

To summarise, indexing is a varied activity with a common core of theory and diverse techniques. In the online environment, the same core of theory applies but techniques need adaptation.

INDEXING ON THE WEB

When online library catalogues and later the Internet appeared, it was thought that automatic indexing would dispense with the need for the 'human touch.' This opinion has proved to be false.[7] Indeed, intellectual indexing, vocabulary control, and structured search techniques have become even more important in electronic data files than in printed files, precisely because of the great size of the databases and the 'genuinely remarkable power of the searching algorithms.'[7] Intellectual indexing processes can be applied in the context of the Internet in order to create useful and efficient signposts.

In the online context, the book indexing approach undergoes the most radical changes. Indexing terms may be stored separately and linked to the relevant parts of the text. More likely, they are put at the front instead of the back, leading in with a hierarchy of terms taking the searcher from the more general to the specific, which is the approach used by classification systems such as Dewey Decimal Classification (DDC).[8] This approach is well suited to the online environment of Web text documents where it is more convenient for the searcher to select from a succession of short lists than to scan one extensive list.

Document indexing for database entry is already adapted to the online environment, and is most efficient within a bibliographic database with an online search function, where retrieval sets are created on a 'one-to-many' basis. For example, a search on 'greenhouse effect' might retrieve 15 references simultaneously. One problem with online text document indexes is that links are on a 'one-to-one' basis. That is to say, one hypertext link leads to one site only, for example, <A HREF="http://www.geocities.com/">The Nomadia Project</A>.

Indexing by human intervention is an 'added value' feature which, ideally, requires a trained indexer and carries associated costs. The dilemma of the Internet is the conflict between the admirable desire to make as much information as possible freely available, and the need for a structured approach to make the information more easily findable. The cost to the searcher consists of time and effort rather than direct charges.[9]

HTML DOCUMENT STRUCTURE

The structure of Internet documents affects signposting and searchability. Text documents marked up in HTML have limited search control compared with bibliographic database fields. Web crawlers may index only the first few sentences or paragraphs. These limitations have led to singular signposting solutions, as we shall see.

THE VARIETY OF SIGNPOSTS

Various kinds of signposts, both automated and manual, have been developed for the Web. Barry[10] identifies the following types of online indexes:

- single server indexes–full text automatic indexes
- multi-host indexes–automatic Web crawlers (such as Harvest)
- global indexes–large Internet search engines with statistical ranking algorithms, and
- selective indexes–quality manual indexing by individual institutions for their own purposes.

Search engines, browsers, crawlers, and robots seek out and create links to Internet resources.

Signposts, as navigation aids, can be categorised in three ways.[11] Firstly, browsing software; secondly, structured guidance to users through classified or categorised approaches to information resources; and, thirdly, information retrieval support through a combination of robot searching software and improved searching functions such as those in Wide Area Information Service (WAIS) databases. The three approaches provide a combination of manual and automatic content analysis and software search capabilities.

Signposts can also be divided into centralised and decentralised indexes.[12] In a central index, everything that is searchable is indexed in one place. Searching is made easier, but gathering information to form the index is more of a challenge. Distributed indexes may be scattered across servers in a hierarchical or non-hierarchical manner, with or without a formalised relationship between indexes. The World Wide Web Virtual Library is an example of a linked, distributed resource. Indeed, a 'virtual library' may be defined as a distributed electronic index or catalogue providing subject access to networked bibliographic documents, resources, and information systems.

Yet again, signposts can be divided into 'external' and 'internal' indexes. External signposts are indexes to remote sites which can be created by the searcher using browser bookmarks or a Web document held on the local computer. Internal signposts can be created inside the documents themselves by the author, or in a set of documents stored together at a Web site. Signposts can be rudimentary, for example, a list of bookmarks, or complex and analytical of subject content, for example, a structured page of links, transferable to the user's Web pages.

EXTERNAL SIGNPOSTS

External signposts can be formed when robot-driven search engines, such as AltaVista and Infoseek, explore Web sites and extract data from documents. The result of a search by a search engine is a 'vacant,' or 'vacuum' index, meaning that it is a temporary listing. While it can be downloaded to form the basis for a local index, it does not exist outside the search. Virtual libraries, on the other hand, form more lasting indexes to Web materials.

Bookmarks provide access at the document level, that is, to the beginning of the document. Once the document is open at the bookmark, the searcher must navigate within the document to find specific items of information. Bookmarks are external signposts contained within browsers, such as Netscape and Internet Explorer, stored on the user's own computer. The searcher can add new bookmarks to keep track of useful Web sites. These may be sorted and edited, depending on the version of the browser. The bookmarks are created from the document title which appears in the top bar of the browser window. For ready identification, they rely on the author of Web documents providing meaningful titles in the head section of the document.

The searcher can also create an index of Web resources as a document on the local computer. The links can be at the document level or take the searcher directly to specific parts of documents using 'anchors,' which are denoted by a hash symbol or '#', for example, <A HREF="http://www.geocities.com/SunsetStrip/8200/books.html# Biography general">Elvis Books</A>.

This index can be created by the searcher, either as a new document, by editing the browser bookmarks file, or downloading and tailoring an existing Web site document. Examples of online indexes are supplied in Appendix A.

INTERNAL SIGNPOSTS

Internal signposts are indexing terms stored inside documents, making them more accessible for searching. As already mentioned, the title in the header of an HTML document forms the bookmark for the searcher. Therefore, the naming of the title is important for the bookmark file, and its creation should be treated to some extent as an indexing function by the author of the Web document.

Metadata is a particular kind of internal signposting and one which is assuming increasing importance. A metadata record consists of a set of elements, sometimes called fields or attributes, which describe different parts of a resource. This information forms a multi-field index/ catalogue record. Metadata is added to the head of an HTML document to provide indexing which is not usually displayed, but is useful information, accessible to search engines such as crawlers and robots for generating automatic Web indexes. The inclusion of metadata in a document contributes to improved precision in search results. Unfortunately, some search engines do not support metadata, for example, Lycos and Northern Light, and very few use metadata for ranking purposes.[13]

In the metadata example below, 'DC' stands for 'Dublin Core.' The 15[14] core elements cover: Title, Author or Creator, Subject and Keywords, Description, Publisher, Other Contributor, Date Created/Modified, Resource Type, Format, Resource Identifier, Source, Language, Relation, Coverage, Rights Management. Not all elements may be used in any particular metadata record.

<META NAME='DC.Title' LANG='en' CONTENT='Signposts on the Information Superhighway'>
<META NAME='DC.Creator' LANG='en' CONTENT='Susan Mac-Dougall'>
<META NAME='DC.Subject' LANG='en' CONTENT='World Wide Web; Information access; Subject indexing; Vocabulary control; Metadata'>
<META NAME='DC.Description' LANG='en' CONTENT='Vocabulary control would improve information retrieval on the World Wide Web.'>
<META NAME='DC.Publisher' LANG='en' CONTENT='Journal of Internet Cataloging'>
<META NAME='DC.Date' LANG='en' CONTENT='990528'>
<META NAME='DC.Type' LANG='en' CONTENT='Document'>
<META NAME='DC.Format' LANG='en' CONTENT='Text/HTML'>
<META NAME='DC.Rights' LANG='en' CONTENT='s'>

Several Web sites offer metadata entry and editing forms which can be filled in and then e-mailed to the author. Some metadata resources are listed in Appendix B. Deacon[15] also provides an example where metadata for a PDF (Portable Document Format) document can be founded embedded in an HTML cover page:

<http://www.health.gov.au/pubs/injury/index.htm>

Metadata can serve several purposes. It can be used as a document surrogate—an alternative catalogue or index record describing a resource, held outside the document. Software already exists on the Web to convert between Dublin Core metadata and MARC formats. Appendix C shows one such online conversion. Metadata can also provide the basis for a 'stocktake' of resources and access to non-electronic resources.[16] However, metadata is labour intensive and requires training.

The Dublin Core metadata schema[17] is one of several, but looks set to become an international standard. Development parties and working teams still meet to refine the meta tags. Originally, simplicity was pursued, with the intention that authors should provide their own tags. However, even with online assistance in the form of drop down lists, validation, spell checking, and copy and paste, the process appears complicated and daunting, and so professional indexers may be required to prepare the tags. This is one area in which cataloguers have shown great interest, and where there is an opportunity for expanding the tasks of cataloguers into the online environment.

Thus, signposts can be outside or within HTML documents, created by document authors, Web indexers, or individual searchers. They include browser bookmarks, indexes, hypertext-activated lists, directories and metadata. Metadata can also be used outside the original document as a document surrogate, linking to the full-text document itself.

SIGNPOSTING WITH CONTROLLED VOCABULARIES

There is a growing interest[18] in the use of controlled vocabularies and classification schemes on the Internet. Current retrieval problems are often a result of limited search engine capabilities and use of natural language. Compared with some other information sources, the Internet has limited points of entry, a lack of structure, but a strong emphasis on subject searching.[19] In the past, Web search capabilities were fairly rudimentary. Now, the situation has improved. The major search engines now allow the use of the Boolean 'AND', 'OR' and 'NOT', truncation, phrase searching, and document searching by area, such as title or text. The default 'OR' can cause confusion.

It is generally accepted that do-it-yourself searchers tend not to take full advantage of advanced search features. Failure to do produces inappropriate degrees of recall and precision. The results are too many hits, false drops, and too many items of limited relevance. At the same time, relevant items may be missed. Keyword searching, that is, searching on individual natural language words, is user-dependent and culture-specific, and therefore a 'hit and miss' affair.[19] Searching on a controlled vocabulary, on the other hand, is not. If indexing terms are controlled and cross-referenced with entry terms to lead the user to the preferred term, even the unsophisticated searcher should achieve better search results.

Thus, Internet indexing with a controlled vocabulary is not only possible, but highly desirable to improve the efficiency of searching. A good thesaurus provides vocabulary control complete with definitions, structure, including hierarchies, synonyms, and a display of relationships. Some thesauri available over the Web are listed in Appendix D.

Library classification schemes and many thesauri employ a numeric, or alphanumeric, code to represent subjects structured hierarchically from broad to narrow, general to specific. The broad-to-narrow approach suits the Internet. Rather than selecting from a long list of specific terms involving scrolling through a long document, the user first selects a broad category, then is guided to more specific terms. An example of a broad-to-narrow subject index is supplied in Appendix E. If a classification code is used, the end-user requires specialist knowledge. One possible application of a classification code is in a multi-lingual environment, used as a conversion code to map between different languages. Thus, thesauri and classification schemes can assist vocabulary control to improve retrieval on the Web, reducing frustration and helping to ensure that useful information is not lost.

GOOD SIGNPOSTING

Good signposting involves useful links, careful selection of terminology and a logical structure.

While some sources on evaluation of Internet and Web resources concentrate mainly on the content, others also consider aspects of the design and usability of Web sites. McMurdo[20] suggests that Web page authors should consciously plan for the indexing and retrieval of their documents. If the local server on which the Web pages are stored has its own search engine, the authors should provide a search capability. He also suggests that, by using metadata tags, Web authors have an opportunity to influence actively how their documents are described in the output of searches and in the keywords used to index them. The concern is how far individual authors of Web pages will carry out indexing of their own pages, and with what degree of expertise. If Web page authors are part of an organisation there is more likely to be a commitment to making the pages more accessible. Organisations which set up Web pages usually have staff expertise in the form of a Web master who is responsible for the Web site.

The Australian Society of Indexers offers an annual prize for the best online index. The guidelines[21] for judging this competition provide an indication of the criteria for a good online index. These are:

1. *Size*
   at least 100 links

2. *An index* can be:
   a. a Web index–it points to the Web at large
   b. an Intranet index
   c. an online book index
   d. an index of offline information accessible via a Web database
   e. a category index of bibliographies mounted on the Web site

3. *Structure and presentation*
   a. good navigation, e.g., alphabetic list, icons, image maps, multimedia, wallpaper
   b. possible cross references
   c. use of keyword search engines can complement the structure list in (3)
   d. use of metadata tags

4. *Quality*
   links must point to valuable information and be weeded if they break or change their focus

5. *User access*
   a. it must be intuitive and user-friendly
   b. the user must be able to find what they [sic] are looking for within, say, 5 to 10 minutes
   c. users give positive feedback about its usefulness
   d. it ties in with a specific need for information in the user community–not abstract

6. *Semantics*
   a. choice of indexing terms must be broad and easy to browse
   b. the index needs to be focused and well-rounded on a particular area

7. *Techniques*
   a. manual
   b. database

Notable requirements are that signposts can be alphabetic lists, icons, or image maps, that is, textual or visual in format. The choice of indexing terms must be both broad and focused, and contain an adequate breadth and depth of terminology to cover a particular subject area. Metadata tags are also required. There is no specific mention of vocabulary control or thesaurus use save in the possibility of cross referencing. Nor is there mention of pre-Internet criteria used for evaluating indexing and retrieval, such as specificity, exhaustivity, recall, and precision. However, 5.d) appears to relate to relevance. Overall, the criteria are relatively unsophisticated, indicating the underdeveloped nature of conventions for Internet indexing.

Good signposting has as its aim improved retrieval of relevant information. At the same time, the creation of a substantial index involves a great deal of intellectual effort. The development of vocabulary control standards should draw on existing information storage and retrieval theory. If a thesaurus exists on a specialised subject area it should be considered as the basis for a relevant subject index. This body of knowledge should not be re-invented but adapted and further developed. One suggestion is that there should be more emphasis on synonym matching/mapping between terms and closer involvement with search engine developers. [19] Some online thesauri are listed in Appendix D.

PROBLEMS AND ISSUES

The World Wide Web is inherently anarchical and global in nature, crossing national and jurisdictional boundaries. There is a general lack of control and standards and an inability to impose them. Any standards that are developed can probably only be guidelines, with voluntary adherence by authors and/or indexers of Web documents.

Thus, there are ongoing issues of signposting language particularly in specialised subject areas:

- the quality of Internet information
- publishers' attitudes to intellectual indexing
- who decides what should be indexed

- who provides the signposts
- who funds the provision of signposts
- vocabulary control standards
- desirability of a mega-thesaurus, by which is meant a large, all-inclusive thesaurus intended to replace multiple smaller specialised thesauri

CONCLUSION

In conclusion, rapid and efficient access to information depends on a number of factors, including indexing quality and search software capabilities. The case has been argued for intellectual indexing by indexers and cataloguers using controlled vocabularies to compensate for the inadequacies of automatic keyword indexing. Thesauri are as yet little used but could save Internet indexing time and improve retrieval. The most promising use for thesauri is in metadata but thesauri could be used in the creation of any subject index.

Indexes, or signposts, are the links between the information and the information seeker. The signposts must exist and they must be effective. What does it matter how relevant or useful information is if it is inaccessible?

NOTES

1. James D. Anderson, "Education for Indexing in North America: Course Content, Emphasis, and Approach," *Indexer* 13:2 (Oct 1982): 92-100.

2. Cherryl Schauder, "An educational role for the Australian Society of Indexers," *Indexer* 18:1 (April 1992): 22.

3. Australian Society of Indexers ACT Region Branch, *Indexing Education and Training in Australia: A Project of the Australian Society of Indexers ACT Region Branch* (Canberra: AusSI, 1998)

4. F.W. Lancaster, *Indexing and Abstracting in Theory and Practice* (Champaign IL: University of Illinois, 1991), p. 15.

5. *Anglo-American Cataloguing Rules*, 2nd ed., rev. 1998, M. Gorman, ed. (Chicago IL: American Library Association, 1998).

6. *Library of Congress Subject Headings in Microform*, (Washington DC: Library of Congress, 1992 -).

7. T.G. McFadden, "Indexing the Internet," *Learned Publishing* 7:1 (Jan 1994): 25.

8. Melvil Dewey, *Dewey Decimal Classification and Relative Index*, 4 v., 20th ed. (Albany NY: Forest Press, 1989).

9. Susan MacDougall, "Rethinking Indexing: The Impact of the Internet," *Australian Library Journal* 45:4 (Nov 1996): 281-285.

10. Tony Barry, "Will Indexers be Redundant by the Year 2005?" paper presented at *The Futureproof Indexer*, Australian Society of Indexers (Katoomba NSW, 27-28 Sep 1997).

11. Michael Middleton, "Indexing the Internet," in *Indexers - Partners in Publishing: Proceedings from the First International Conference, Friday March 31 to Sunday April 2, 1995, Marysville, Victoria Australia*, Australian Society of Indexers, M.J. McMaster, ed., (Melbourne: AusSI, 1995), p. 196-205.

12. *Indexing the Web* <http://www.hypernews.org/HyperNews/get/hypernews/evolution.html> (31 May 1996) Seen 26 May 1999.

13. *Search Engine Features Chart* <http://www.searchenginewatch.com/webmasters/ features.html> (Date unknown) Seen 26 May 1999.

14. *Dublin core Metadata Element Set: Reference Description* <http://purl.oclc.org/dc/about/element_set.htm> (2 February 1997) Seen 26 May 1999.

15. Prue Deacon, "Use of Metadata in the Department of Health and Family Services," paper presented at *Metadata Unravelled: Developments for the Information Professional* (Canberra, 26-27 Aug 1998).

16. National Archives of Australia. Office of Government Information Technology. *The Australian Government Locator Service (AGLS) Manual for users, version: 1998-07-27* [metadata] (Canberra: AGLS, 1998).

17. "Metadata Tools and Services" <http://metadata.net> (23 July 1998) Seen 26 May 1999.

18. Prue Deacon, "Use of the Human Services Thesaurus in Metadata," paper presented at *Metadata Unravelled: Developments for the Information Professional* (Canberra, 26-27 Aug 1998). The thesaurus is available online at URL <http://www.health.gov.au:80/archive/1999/thesauru/thesaur.htm> (April 1995) Seen 26 May 1999.

19. Lynn Farkas, "Subject Analysis on the Internet: Issues in Thesaurus Use," notes for presentation at the *Metadata Unravelled: Developments for the Information Professional* (Canberra, 26-27 Aug 1998).

20. George McMurdo, "Evaluating Web Information and Design," *Journal of Information Science*, 24:3 (1998).

21. Dwight Walker, personal communication (15 July 1998).

APPENDIX A
(Links current May 1999)

Examples of Large and Multiple Indexes

All-in-One Search
  <http://www.AllOneSearch.dom/>
CUSI: Common Interface to WWW Search Engines
  <http://www.telstra.com.au/index/cusi.html>
Find-it! Internet Tools
  <http://www.iTools.com/find-it.html>
Profusion
  <http://profusion.com/>

Examples of Subject Guides

Clearinghouse: Subject-Oriented Internet Resource Guides
  <http://www.clearinghouse.net/>
Subject-oriented Web Indexing
  <http://godzilla.zeta.org.au/%7Eaussi/webindexing/links.htm#
subject-oriented lists>
The WWW Virtual Library
  <http://vlib.org/>

Geographic Index

The Asian Studies WWW Virtual Library
  <http://coombs.anu.edu.au/WWWVL-AsianStudies.html>

Information on Search Engines

Annotated Guide to WWW Search Engines
  <http://www.ciolek.com/SearchEngines.html>
Search Engine Features Chart
  <http://www.searchenginewatch.com/webmasters/features.html>
Searching the Internet
  <http://anulib.anu.edu/elibrary/search.html>

APPENDIX B
(Links current May 1999)

Online Metadata Resources

How to Use Meta Tags
  <http://www.searchenginewatch.com/webmasters/meta.html>
Meta Matters
  <http://www.nla.gov.au/meta/>
Meta Tags can Index, Organise your Web pages
  <http://www8.zdnet.com/pcweek/ir/0113/13jia.html>
Metadata Tools and Services, including Reggie–the Metadata Editor
  <http://metadata.net>
d2m: Dublin Core to MARC (MAchine-Readable Catalogue) converter
  <http://www.bibsys.no/meta/d2m/>
Metadata: Mapping Between Metadata Formats
  <http://www.ukoln.ac.uk/>

Metadata tag specifying Environment Australia Thesaurus:
<META NAME='DC.Subject' SCHEME='Environment Australia Thesaurus
http://www.environment.gov.au/library/ea_thesaurus.html' CONTENT= 'Information Technologies'>

APPENDIX C

Metadata Record Before Automatic Conversion to USMARC

<META NAME= "DC.date" CONTENT="(TYPE=current) (SCHEME=ISO31)
1999-05-24">
<META NAME="DC.title" CONTENT="Asian Studies WWW Virtual Li-
brary">
<META NAME="DC.creator" CONTENT="(TYPE=name) Dr T.Matthew Cio-
lek">
<META NAME="DC.creator" CONTENT="(TYPE=email) tmciolek@coombs.
anu.edu.au">
<META NAME="DC.creator" CONTENT="(TYPE=affiliation) The Australian
National University">
<META NAME="DC.subject" CONTENT="Asian Studies online resources cat-
alog">
<META NAME="DC.description" CONTENT="An annotated Internet guide to
Asian Studies">
<META NAME="DC.date" CONTENT="(TYPE=creation)(SCHEME=ISO31)
1994-03-24">

<META NAME="DC.type" CONTENT="Service">
<META NAME="DC.format" CONTENT="(SCHEME=imt) text/html">
<META NAME="DC.identifier" CONTENT="(TYPE=url) http://coombs. anu.edu.au/WWWVL-AsianStudies.html">
<META NAME="DC.language"CONTENT="(SCHEME=NISOZ39.53) ENG">
<META NAME="DC.coverage" CONTENT="Asian continent, countries and regions">
<META NAME="keywords" content="APEC, ASEAN, Asia-Pacific, Middle East, Caucasus, Central Asia, South Asia, South East Asia, Australia, New Zealand, Pacific Ocean, East Asia, Afghanistan, Armenia, Assyria, Australia, Azerbaijan, Bahrain, Bangladesh, Bhutan, Brunei, Burma, Cambodia, Chechnya, China, East Timor, Eastern Turkistan, . . . ">
<META NAME="description" content="Asian Studies WWW Virtual Library">

Resulting USMARC Record

008990526s1999
245 $a Asian Studies WWW Virtual Library
700 $a Dr T.Matthew Ciolek
653 $a Asian Studies online resources catalog
500 $a Asian continent, countries and regions
260 $c 1999
856 $u http://coombs.anu.edu.au/WWWVL-AsianStudies.html $q text/html

Source: <http://coombs.anu.edu.au/WWWVL-AsianStudies.html> (1994) Seen May 1999.

APPENDIX D
(Links current May 1999)

Online Thesauri

Getty Museum's Art and Architecture Thesaurus (AAT)
  <http://shiva.pub.getty.edu/aat.browser/>
Human Services Thesaurus, 3rd edition
  <http://www.health.gov.au:80/archive/1999/thesauru/thesaur.htm>
ITS (Intelligent Transportation Systems) thesaurus
  <http://www.nas.edu/trb/about/pathesau.html>
NASA Thesaurus
  <http://www.sti.nasa.gov/thesfrm1.htm>

APPENDIX E

Example of broad-to-narrow subject indexing from the WWW Virtual Library at <http://vlib.org/>. Topics are put into categories and a guide to the contents supplied.

•*Agriculture*
  Agriculture, Beer & Brewing, Gardening . . .

•*Business and Economics*
  Economics, Finance, Transportation . . .

•*Computer Science*
  Computing, Languages, Web . . .

•*Communications and Media*
  Communications, Telecommunications, Journalism . . .

•*Education*
  Education, Cognitive Science, Libraries, Linguistics . . .

•*Engineering*
  Civil, Chemical, Electrical, Mechanical, Software . . .

•*Humanities*
  Anthropology, Art, Dance, History, Museums, Philosophy . . .

•*Information Management*
  Information Sciences, Knowledge Management . . .

•*International Affairs*
International Security, Sustainable Development, UN . . .

•*Law*
Law, Environmental Law . . .

•*Recreation*
Recreation and games, Gardening, Sport . . .

•*Regional Studies*
Asian, Latin American, West European . . .

•*Science*
Biosciences, Health, Earth Science, Physics, Chemistry . . .

•*Society*
Political Science, Religion, Social Sciences . . .

Search Engines
for the World Wide Web:
An Evaluation
of Recent Developments

Sarah J. Clarke

SUMMARY. Search engines are defined, and recent developments described, exemplified, and evaluated, especially those concerned with traditional search and retrieval capabilities. Discussion concentrates on two broad issues: (1) collection and indexing methods and (2) retrieval and ranking methods. It is concluded that a wider adoption of field searching, proximity searching, and relevance feedback would improve quality of search results. *[Article copies available for a fee from The Haworth Document Delivery Service: 1-800-342-9678. E-mail address: getinfo@ haworthpressinc.com <Website: http://www.haworthpressinc.com>]*

KEYWORDS. Search engines, World Wide Web, Internet, information retrieval, evaluation

INTRODUCTION

Search engines have been developed in response to the need for information retrieval on the World Wide Web. Search engines are Web

Sarah J. Clarke is Multimedia Service Development Officer, Open University Library, Milton Keynes, MK7 6HH, England (Sarah.Clarke@open.ac.uk).

[Haworth co-indexing entry note]: "Search Engines for the World Wide Web: An Evaluation of Recent Developments." Clarke, Sarah J. Co-published simultaneously in *Journal of Internet Cataloging* (The Haworth Information Press, an imprint of The Haworth Press, Inc.) Vol. 2, No. 3/4, 2000, pp. 81-93; and: *Internet Searching and Indexing: The Subject Approach* (ed: Alan R. Thomas, and James R. Shearer) The Haworth Information Press, an imprint of The Haworth Press, Inc., 2000, pp. 81-93. Single or multiple copies of this article are available for a fee from The Haworth Document Delivery Service [1-800-342-9678, 9:00 a.m. - 5:00 p.m. (EST). E-mail address: getinfo@haworthpressinc.com].

81

databases that automatically compile their indexes. Search engines work by dispatching programs, commonly described as robots, spiders, or crawlers to collect Web pages. The spider program locates pages by following hypertext links. Once the spider program has located Web pages, it downloads and examines them, extracting indexing information that can be used to describe their content.

Individual search engines employ different algorithms to extract data and build indexes. Techniques may involve simply locating most of the words as they appear on the Web pages or require the performance of statistical analyses to identify key words and phases. These data are then stored in the search engine's database along with the address (URL–Uniform Resource Locator) of the Web page. A user submits a query to the database using a browser program, such as Netscape or Internet Explorer. The search engine produces a list of Web pages including their URLs, which can be clicked on in order to retrieve the Web page.

Since 1994 many competing search services have appeared. Search engines enable users to access information on the Web and therefore search engines are amongst the most popular Web sites. The popularity of search engines has meant that they hold considerable commercial value. They can generate revenue directly from advertisements appearing on their pages, and also through selling their software to other organizations for use as a search tool on their own Web sites or Intranets. These factors result in a very competitive market place for search engine companies. Search engine providers are constantly developing their services in a bid to remain competitive and to attract more visitors to their pages.

A recent general trend is for search engines to become "portals." Steve Shipside[1] describes the portal as being a kind of "everyman's home page." The search engine Web page should become your first port of call, the place where you start every voyage on the Web and the place you go back to every time you need to find something. The search engine or portal companies want their site to become the one-stop shop for all your information needs. As a result search engines are continuing to offer straight Web searching, but in addition are offering increased content provision including directory services, live channels, personalization options, free e-mail, free Web space, free horoscopes, free news, and other goodies. In return the user is expected to answer a few simple questions which helps the search engine company to build up market share, databases and sales pitch. A prime example is Excite which now has horoscopes on its Web site, free e-mail and news under Top Stories, Business, Technology and Sports, and personalization options. InfoSeek is another example of a search engine making developments in this area. Go Network has been developed as a result of the partnership between Disney and InfoSeek. According to Jesse Berst[2] "hubs" and "home bases" may soon replace portals. Berst defines a "hub" as a central position from which everything radiates. A "home base" is an extension of the idea of a personalized search engine page, the aim being that the "home base" is your own area of the Web that you always come back to before you seek more information. This is in contrast to a portal that acts as a gateway that passes you through to other destinations.

The Search Engine Watch Web site by Danny Sullivan[3] is probably the best resource at the moment for those who are interested in monitoring how individual search engines work and the financial and strategic issues that affect their services. The Search Engine Showdown pages by Greg Notess[4] are another useful source of reviews of individual search engines. Traugott Koch[5] has developed a large bibliography on the subject of search engines. Search engines will be evaluated here under two broad categories: Collection and indexing methods and retrieval and ranking methods. The URLs of the search engines and other services mentioned are listed at the end of this paper.

COLLECTION AND INDEXING METHODS

Search Engine Size

No search engine has the capability to index the entire Web and then serve the information back to the whole world.[6] In any case, how much more useful is a search engine that contains 100 million pages as opposed to 80 million? If these 'missing' 20 million pages consist of multiple copies of the same pages, dynamically generated documents, scripts, personalized news pages, shopping baskets using cookies and other such ephemera, then the searcher clearly isn't missing anything too important. However, it is obviously of greater concern if large areas of the Web are being excluded. Search engine companies frequently promote the size of their index, seemingly viewing size of the index as an important indicator as to the quality of their search facility. There are conflicting reports about which search engine has the biggest index and the situation changes frequently.

However, it is interesting to consider the large-scale search engine experiment (over 10,000 queries) by Bharat and Broder,[7] as this illustrates how individual search engines must be employing some kind of "collections policy" to select pages for inclusion in the index. Bharat and Broder estimated that as of November 1997 the approximate sizes of HotBot, AltaVista, Excite, and InfoSeek expressed relative to their joint total coverage at that time, were respectively 48%, 62%, 20% and 17%. Using data from other sources, they estimated that the number of pages indexed by HotBot, AltaVista, Excite, and InfoSeek were respectively 77 million, 100 million, 32 million, and 17 million: 226 million indexed pages overall, with a joint total coverage of 160 million. They also conjectured that the size of the static, public Web at that time was about 200 million, although they also commented that the true size may be much larger than this. What is most startling about their estimates is that only 1.4% of Web pages in the experiment "intersected" with all four of the search engines. This translates as an overlap of only 2.2 million pages.

It is difficult to account for this apparently low overlap of Web pages between search engines. It may be related to the disparity in the collection methods that search engines use. It is also very difficult, due to the size of the search engines and the unknown size of the Web, to determine through experiments what the coverage is of individual search engines. Also, due to the competition between search engines, a search engine company will not want to reveal the exact contents of its index. The algorithms used are highly prized proprietary information. For those concerned about the seemingly discrete coverage of individual search engines, the answer may be to use meta search services, which will query several search engines at once. Examples are Inference Find, SavvySearch, and Go2Net (formerly Metacrawler).

Page Collection Methods

There are two main collection methods by which Web pages can end up in the index of a search engine. They can either be submitted by the creators of Web pages via the "Add URL" features of search engines, or they can be non-submitted (automatically collected and indexed by a spider program). Most search engines do not index all of the pages of a Web site. For example a search engine may index only the top level Web pages such as the homepages. Lycos, InfoSeek, and WebCrawler are search engines that don't gather all the Web pages within an individual Web site. AltaVista, Excite, HotBot, and Northern Light on the other hand do not limit the number of Web pages that are indexed at an individual site. This disparity in the depth of Web pages that are indexed may account for the lack of overlap between search engines. The fact that certain spider programs select only some Web pages may not be a great problem for those searching for information, although it is probably of greater concern to those who are using their Web site as a marketing tool.

Currency of Pages

The currency of the pages collected by the spider is of concern to Web searchers and Webmasters alike. Webmasters are the people responsible for building, designing, and managing a Web site. Dead links, transferred pages, and pages advertising long past events are an irritation to users, whilst Webmasters want to ensure that up-to-date information about their organisation is contained in the index of a search engine. The frequency with which a spider will return to a Web site varies from 1 day to a couple of months, with the more popular pages being visited more frequently. Some search engines which can detect those pages which change most frequently visit such pages more often than more static Web pages. There is also a delay between when the spider collects the page and when its URL actually appears in the index (ranging from 1 day to a couple of months). Non-submitted or spidered pages tend to have a longer time delay than submitted pages.

Excluded Pages

Submitted Web pages can be excluded as a penalty for "spamming" or "spamdexing." Spamdexing is a set of techniques that are used to give Web pages a good ranking in the search engines' result lists. Spamdexing techniques include repeating keywords (which may be unrelated to the page's content), hidden keywords (using small fonts or different colour text), and repeated submissions of the same URL or multiple URLs from the same Web site. Search engines have become wise to spamdexing and now reject submitted pages if they detect spamdexing. AltaVista, Excite, HotBot, InfoSeek, and Lycos all have "spam" penalties.

The collection of Web pages by a search engine can also be affected by Webmasters' decision to block the spider or robot from certain Web pages. A robots.txt text file can be used to keep files and/or directories off limits. In addition, search engines are not able to index such material as Adobe PDF or other formatted files, information held on Intranets, password protected sites, or commercial sites which may limit by domain name or IP address, and non-Web resources. Frames, image maps, and dynamically generated pages can all cause information to be missed.

Indexing

As well as selecting different pages to index, individual search engines will use different methods to index the pages within a Web site. Whether a search engine indexes the whole or only part of the text on a page has an impact on the relevancy of the search results. Excite is a full text index. AltaVista indexes only the first 100K of text, then just the links in the next 4MB of text. Lycos used to index only selected portions of text but now indexes the full text of Web pages. Most search engines remove stop words in order to reduce the size of the index and to speed up searches.

RETRIEVAL AND RANKING METHODS

Text Retrieval

Features that allow users to limit their searches are extremely important when searching a database the size of a search engine. Over the last couple of years, search engines have improved the range of ways in which it is possible to limit a search and reduce the noise in search results. Most search engines support phrase searching, proximity searching, and have Boolean capabilities. HotBot, Northern Light, and AltaVista also allow the user to limit by the date of the Web page. This is a valuable option as it can help overcome the problem of dead and out-of-date links. Truncation is less widely supported. HotBot, which has a range of options for limiting searches, does not offer an option for truncation. A number of search engines will automatically recognize plurals. This can be useful although it inevitably increases noise in the search results. This is especially a problem if it is not possible to turn this feature off. InfoSeek and Lycos are search engines that automatically stem words. However, the use of a full stop or period at the end of a word in Lycos will turn off the automatic stemming. Another way of overcoming this is to surround keywords with quotes to search them as an exact phrase.

The way individual search engines support features such as phrase or Boolean searching varies. Some expect the user to type the relevant syntax. Fortunately there seems to be an increasingly common set of syntax employed by search engines. AltaVista, Excite and Lycos all use double quotation marks to denote phrases (e.g., "tax reform"), + to denote the required operator (e.g., +Africa), and − the prohibited operator (e.g., − Asia). Alternatively, many search engines provide menus and boxes that can be used to limit the searches. HotBot in particular favours this approach. This is useful in that it saves the users from having to check the help files of search engines to check what syntax the system uses. Help files can take a long time to download, an irritant for those who need to find information quickly.

Muscat EuroFerret has the added advantage of not requiring the user to enter anything in the way of Boolean commands or required/prohibited operators. Instead, users are encouraged to type in a large number of appropriate words to describe the query. Natural language processing options like this have great potential for improving the relevancy of results for inexperienced searchers. Natural language processing relieves users of deciding which search commands to use for each search engine, and it allows them to formulate an effective search topic in the form of a question. However, there are some problems with these systems in that they, not the users, provide the search logic. In some cases, both AND and OR links between terms would be sensible, and the machine may "decide" wrongly. Either of the search statements *Africa OR Asia* or *Africa AND Asia* could be appropriate depending on the context that at present only a human would understand.

Field searching is a powerful tool for ensuring relevant search results. AltaVista, HotBot, InfoSeek, and Lycos all offer some field searching options. HotBot and AltaVista offer the most extensive range of field searching options including the ability to search by title, URL (including domain and host), language (AltaVista), continent (HotBot). Retrieval of images is discussed below. Ran Hock[8] provides a detailed review of field searching using search engines.

AltaVista has the added feature of recognizing Real Names in its Simple Mode. A user can type in the name of an organization or brand name and as long as this company has registered as a Real Name then the Real Name Address link will be displayed first. To those users who want to find the homepage of a well-known company it can be annoying to be given a list of Web pages *about* that company. Real Name helps to solve these problems for the user.

Ranking

The way search engines rank search results is very important to the end-user. Most users will only have the time or patience to evaluate the top ten or twenty Web pages that are returned by a particular search. Therefore the effectiveness of the ranking algorithm in matching Web pages to the query is crucial to user satisfaction. The details of how individual search engines rank their pages are not published, given the proprietary nature of these systems. However, most search engines use the same general principles. Location of the keyword or phrase is the most important factor. If the keyword or phrase is contained in the title page or near the top of the Web page then that page will be ranked more highly. The inclusion of keywords in the meta tags may also increase the ranking. Although InfoSeek and HotBot give a boost to Web pages that have keywords in their meta tags, some search engines such as Excite do not examine meta tags. If a keyword occurs frequently in a page then this will also give the Web page a higher ranking. Where a large number of keywords or phrases are included in the query, the pages that contain a required word or phrase will be ranked first. If no required words are specified, then the pages that contain all of the words will be ranked first. In AltaVista's Advanced Mode results are not ranked, unless one or more terms are selected for special weighting at the beginning of the search.

In some cases, the popularity of the Web page is also a factor. WebCrawler, for example, will rank a page more highly according to link popularity. That is, if other pages frequently link to a page then it will be ranked more highly. In some cases, if the search engine has a reviewed or directory service, then pages which are listed in this directory will be ranked more highly. The popularity of a link or whether it has been reviewed may not be the most important factor to the user. They may be more interested in whether the subject of the Web page matches their query, particularly if they are trying to find information on a very specific topic.

A highly ranked page is not necessarily the most relevant to the user. It is simply the page that matches most closely the ranking algorithm of the search engines. The highest ranked pages would ideally be the most relevant pages to the users, but quite commonly non-relevant pages achieve a high rank. This is unsurprising given the volume of information contained in the index of most search engines. These problems may also be due to the user not utilizing the search facilities of the particular engine properly, or by not entering enough keywords to describe their query. One way in which search engines can help the user to increase the relevancy of the results is to use relevance feedback. AltaVista has a Refine button that allows the user to refine a search. A list of the keywords found in the retrieved Web pages is shown and the percentage of pages in which these keywords occur is also listed. The user can mark the keywords that are most relevant and then run another search using these as the specification for further retrieval. Similarly, Muscat EuroFerret employs relevance feedback by allowing users to mark the retrieved Web pages that are most relevant, and then uses these Web pages as the specification for further retrieval.

Image Retrieval

Search engines are primarily concerned with text retrieval. Over the last couple of years a number of search engines have developed services which allow users to search and retrieve images on the World Wide Web. Indexing and then retrieving images presents problems additional to those of text retrieval.

A textual document describes its own content and it is possible to search the words of the document. In order to search for images the image has to be described textually. While there are some experimental systems that allow queries by image content, current public search engines use the textual approach. Paula Berinstein[9] reviews and evaluates a number of search engines for image retrieval. The most common strategy employed by search engines is to look for Web pages that contain graphics files. They detect files which have both the

HTML tags: IMG SRC (this means "display the following image file") and HREF (this means "the following is a link"), and a filename ending with an image suffix such as .GIF or .JPG. As far as determining the content of the files, a search engine can index the file name itself (e.g., cat.gif) or look at the URL path for the image file name (/pictures/pets/cat.gif). Some search engines can also use captions that describe the image such as the ALT tag, the title tag, and meta tags. The ALT tag is used by Web page creators to describe an image for users who do not have a graphics enabled browser or who turn the browser's graphics display off. In some cases the link to the image may describe the image content. The drawbacks of these methods are that they rely on the person producing the Web page to describe the images in an informative way. File names may often consist of cryptic or abbreviated names.

Thus, for an image search on AltaVista, the user types the word *image:* followed by an appropriate search term. The search engine then examines pages with the HTML IMG SRC tag to determine the presence or otherwise of a .GIF or .JPG file, and then attempts to match the searcher's term to the file or directory name. This approach is fairly rudimentary. A specialized image search engine is WebSEEK from Columbia University. WebSEEK employs an automated agent to collect and index images. Like AltaVista, WebSEEK looks for images and other file types by looking at file extensions, then extracting text from the ALT tag, file name, directory name, and links to the picture. The terms in the extracted text are mapped to subject categories that can be browsed and searched. An additional advantage over the AltaVista approach is that it is possible to preview the images at reduced size–thumbnails. WebSEEK also identifies files with extensions such as .MPG, .AVI and .QT which are used for MPEG, Microsoft, and Quicktime video formats respectively. WebSEEK doesn't appear to identify .BMP or .TIF extensions during its indexing process. WebSEEK does not support phrase searching. HotBot and Lycos are two other major search engines that offer image retrieval. In addition AltaVista has recently introduced a special image, video and audio search service called AltaVista Photo and Media Finder (it is linked from the main AltaVista homepage) which it has developed in conjunction with the Virage Corporation. Virage specializes in video and image search software.

What none of these automated systems can do is enable the user to identify the owner of copyright of any images. Frequently when users retrieve images on the Web, they have to work backwards from the URLs to find out who mounted the image on the Web. It is important to bear in mind that the person who publishes the image on the Web may not be the copyright owner, and that information published on the Web may not be freely reproduced. AltaVista makes this point on the homepage of its Photo and Media Finder service.

Overall the ability to retrieve images using search engines is a useful facility if not their strongest function. Hopefully, these facilities will improve in the future although much will rely on the development of good practice amongst those who design and manage Web pages. Examples of good practice are giving titles to pages, including descriptions and keywords in meta tags, and giving image files informative names either in the file names themselves, in the ALT tag or in the text of links to images. Given the wide variety of media types accessible from the Web, these aspects of the search engines will grow in importance.

CONCLUSION

Considering the volume of data that they index and then search, search engines do a good job in retrieving relevant information from the World Wide Web. However, in order to achieve the best results when searching the Web, it is often necessary to employ a variety of strategies and services. Subject directories such as Yahoo, Newhoo, or the World Wide Web Virtual Library may be a better option for finding information on general topics, finding homepages of organizations, and information on current events. The search engines are more effective when the search employs specific keywords and phrases, and when there is a requirement to find information which may be buried within some of the lower level pages in a Web site. The provision of directory services on the search engines' pages is a welcome development. AltaVista and HotBot both use branded versions of the Look-Smart directory, Lycos has a directory service called "Web Guides" and a review service called "Top 5%", Excite "channels" list sites by topic. InfoSeek and WebCrawler also have their own directories.

An increase in good practice amongst those producing and managing Web pages is part of a solution to improving the text retrieval capabilities of search engines. Simple things like giving pages titles and descriptions in the form of meta tags are an effective way of improving the relevancy of search results, provided the particular engine offers such features. The question is how to encourage Web page creators to adopt these methods. An answer may be for search engines to index only those pages that have been submitted, rather than "spidered" pages, and then only to accept such pages as conform to certain standards. However, this may have an undesirable impact on the breadth of coverage of the search engines because commercial sites are more likely to be more aggressive in submitting pages than academic or research institutions.

Given the huge size of the search engines, features such as phrase searching, field searching, proximity, improved natural language processing, and relevance feedback are very useful to users. Greg Notess[10] suggests that two useful additions would be (1) the ability to track and combine search sets, and (2) for Web search engines to index back files and current issues of free online publications. Northern Light has already taken steps towards the second suggestion by providing a searchable Special Collections database of articles and book reviews, although payment is required in order to obtain the full text of the items (which may sometimes be available free elsewhere). It is to be hoped that search engine companies will concentrate on these kinds of features, thus building improved subject retrieval capabilities.

SEARCH ENGINES AND DIRECTORIES

AltaVista	<URL http://www.altavista.com/>
Excite	<URL: http://www.excite.com/>
Go Network	<URL: http://www.go.com/>
Go2Net	<URL: http://www.go2net.com/>
HotBot	<URL: http://www.hotbot.com/>
Inference Find	<URL: http://www.ifind.com/>
InfoSeek	<URL: http://www.infoseek.com/>
LookSmart	<URL: http://www.looksmart.com/>
Lycos	<URL: http://www.lycos.com/>
Muscat EuroFerret	<URL: http://www.euroferret.com/>
Newhoo	<URL: http://dmoz.org/>
Northern Light	<URL: http://www.northernlight.com/>
SavvySearch	<URL: http://www.savvysearch.com/>
Virage Corporation	<URL: http://www.virage.com/>
WebCrawler	<URL: http://www.webcrawler.com/>

WebSEEK   <URL: http://disney.ctr.columbia.edu/webseek/>
World Wide Web
Virtual Library   <URL: http://vlib.org/>
Yahoo   <URL: http://www.yahoo.com/>

REFERENCES

1. Steve Shipside, "Gateway to Heaven?", *Internet Magazine (UK)* 45 (August 1998): 46-52.

2. Jesse Berst, "What's Next After Portals?", *ZDNet AnchorDesk*
<URL: http://www.zdnet.com/anchordesk/story/story_2263.html> (January 1999) Seen 2 September 1999.

3. Danny Sullivan, "Search Engine Watch"
<URL: http://www.searchenginewatch.com/> (1999) Seen 09 April 1999.

4. Greg Notess, "Search Engine Showdown"
<URL: http://www.notess.com/> (April 1999) Seen 2 September 1999.

5. Traugott Koch, "Literature About Search Services"
<URL: http://www.ub2.lu.se/desire/radar/lit-about-search-services.html> (May 1998) Seen 2 September 1999.

6. David Brake, "Lost in Cyberspace", *New Scientist* 156:2110 (1997): 12-13.

7. Krishna Bharat and Andrei Broder, "A Technique for Measuring the Relative Size and Overlap of Public Web Search Engines", *Computer Networks and ISDN Systems* 30:1-7 (1998): 380.

8. Ran Hock, "How to Do Field Searching in Web Search Engines: A Field Trip"
<URL: http://www.onlineinc.com/onlinemag/OL1998/hock5.html> (May 1998) Seen 2 September 1999.

9. Paula Berinstein, "Turning Visual: Image Search Engines on the Web", *Online* 22:3 (1998): 37-42.

10. Greg Notess, "Looking Ahead to 1998 on the Net"
<URL: http://www.onlineinc.com/onlinemag/OL1998/net1.html> (January 1998) Seen 2 September 1999.

CLASSIFICATION AND ITS CONTRIBUTION TO WEB ORGANIZATION, INDEXING, AND SEARCHING

NET: Anything reticulated or decussated at equal distances, with interstices between the intersections

  −Samuel Johnson, *A Dictionary of the English Language,* 1755

[Where] al is fishe, that cometh to the net

  −George Gascoigne, *The Steele Glass,* 1576

The Relevance of Facet Analysis
for World Wide Web Subject Organization
and Searching

David Ellis
Ana Vasconcelos

SUMMARY. Different forms of indexing and search facilities available on the Web are described. Use of facet analysis to structure hypertext concept structures is outlined in relation to work on (1) development of hypertext knowledge bases for designers of learning materials
and (2) construction of knowledge based hypertext interfaces. The
problem of lack of closeness between page designers and potential users is examined. Facet analysis is suggested as a way of alleviating
some difficulties associated with this problem of designing for the unknown user. *[Article copies available for a fee from The Haworth Document
Delivery Service: 1-800-342-9678. E-mail address: getinfo@haworthpressinc.com
<Website: http://www.haworthpressinc.com>]*

KEYWORDS. Facet analysis, Internet, World Wide Web, information
retrieval, indexing, searching, hypertext, hypermedia

David Ellis, PhD, is Senior Lecturer, Department of Information Studies, University of Sheffield, Sheffield S10 2TN UK (d.ellis@sheffield.ac.uk).
Ana Vasconcelos, BA, MIInfSc, is Senior Lecturer, School of Computing and Management Sciences, Sheffield Hallam University, Sheffield S1 1UB UK (a.c.vasconcelos@
shu.ac.uk).

[Haworth co-indexing entry note]: "The Relevance of Facet Analysis for World Wide Web Subject
Organization and Searching." Ellis, David, and Ana Vasconcelos. Co-published simultaneously in *Journal
of Internet Cataloging* (The Haworth Information Press, an imprint of The Haworth Press, Inc.) Vol. 2, No. 3/4,
2000, pp. 97-114; and: *Internet Searching and Indexing: The Subject Approach* (ed: Alan R. Thomas, and
James R. Shearer) The Haworth Information Press, an imprint of The Haworth Press, Inc., 2000, pp. 97-114.
Single or multiple copies of this article are available for a fee from The Haworth Document Delivery Service
[1-800-342-9678, 9:00 a.m. - 5:00 p.m. (EST). E-mail address: getinfo@haworthpressinc.com].

97

BACKGROUND

The Internet has its origins in a network, called the ARPAnet, developed in the early 1970s by the Advanced Research Projects Agency (ARPA) in the US. At first it was used for the transfer of intelligence within the US Department of Defense, but, later on, it was adopted by the academic community to build an academic network for information exchange.[1,2] By the late 1980s, access to the Net was open to the general public as network technology introduced client server architectures and ethernet local area networks, supporting end-user access to networks. By the mid-1990s, the Internet was made of over 60,000 networks, with a growth rate of 10% per month and an estimated 50 million people worldwide having access to the Internet on e-mail, displaying a growth rate of 1,000% per year of use of file search and retrieval tools.[1] The Internet is a voluntary and cooperative effort, where over 60,000 participating networks agree on the common protocols and rules. Nobody, therefore, is officially in charge of or controls the Internet.

The World Wide Web (or the WWW or the W3) is the multimedia part of the Internet, displaying a hypertext type of structure and search facilities (browsing and navigation). It was first developed for sharing documents between nuclear physicists of the European Particle Physics Laboratory (CERN) in Switzerland, 1989, but the first commercial Web Software, by NeXT, in 1991, soon popularised this form of access to the Internet. The main characteristics of the WWW organisation and structure are:

- organising documents into pieces of information (pages), using a set of rules which tag and format the documents, the Hypertext Markup Language (HTML)
- every individual document or page is assigned an unique address, called the Uniform Resource Locator (URL)
- each URL can be linked with a hypertext type of link to other URLs and even pieces of information within each document (buttons) can be linked to URLs or to other pieces of information
- these documents can be searched through interactive interface programs which allow users to browse and navigate through the documents and are called Web Browsers
- the communication between the Web Browsers and the Web servers is regulated by a common language using a standardised

set of rules called Hypertext Transfer Protocol (HTTP).[1,2] The HTTP allows the interpretation of the HTML signs within each Web page, in order to display correctly the page and to enable the transfer of files.

The huge size of the Internet and its growth rate, together with the fact that there is no control over it, means that:

- a huge volume of information is generated every minute
- no order or rules are imposed on the generation, distribution, access, and use of this information
- no fully comprehensive record of the different documents is available at the moment
- no classification and description framework for storing and retrieving these documents has been commonly accepted and established, although there are several classifications which have been applied to parts of the WWW
- therefore, documents of all kinds of format (text files, sounds, images, video clips), type of information (electronic journals, tourist information, marketing services, commercial sales, library catalogues) and subject (astrology, cookery recipes, satellite images of the Earth, university course guides, government reports, business databases) can be found.

Hypertext is the linking mechanism of the World Wide Web. Ted Nelson[3,4,5,6,7] coined the term 'hypertext,' or nonsequential writing, to refer to non-linear text which it would be inconvenient to produce or represent on paper. The hypertext structure of the Web means that retrieval is done through following the links between different Web pages, through browsing and navigation. Because each Web page will have multiple links, there will be multiple paths to the same piece of information. This way of searching by association has advantages and disadvantages:[8]

- the main advantage is that it can lead to finding information people are not aware of, just by following links
- the main disadvantage is that people usually have to follow different layers of linked information in order to retrieve one specific page or piece of information
- with the huge increase of the WWW–which doubles its size every four months[9]–the problems associated with this way of

searching for information are increased, since there is no comprehensive framework which guides the organisation of the Web. As stressed by Tyner,[10] searching for a specific piece of information through the over 150 million pages on the Web without a central catalogue becomes an almost impossible task.

Although the WWW does not have a central catalogue or index, different search tools have been devised in order to assist people in finding information on the largest repository of documents in the world. These search tools can be divided into two main categories: subject directories and search engines.

SUBJECT DIRECTORIES

Subject directories (also called subject trees or subject guides) allow people to browse information by subject, such as Accounting and Finance, Astrology, Biology, Health. They are hierarchically organised indexes of different subjects, with links to different Web sites on each subject. The searcher can browse through the index in search of relevant subjects and navigate to the relevant Web sites, by clicking on hotspots which represent those sites. Subject directories are built by human indexers using indexing and abstracting techniques. Editors constantly review sites, index them, and build short descriptions of these sites. Alternatively, Web site producers submit their own description of their sites to the organisations which compile these indexes.

These short descriptions are maintained in the subject directory database and linked to the main index. The descriptions usually provide a link to the Home page of a Web site, rather than a link to each individual page in a site. The fact that the links are made to the top level of Web sites means that subject directories are better adjusted to searching general subjects. Because they are humanly indexed, subject directories tend to retrieve more relevant information than other search tools. However, their drawback is that they take some time to include new sites in their indexes and in reviewing these new sites. Examples of subject directories include: *Galaxy (http://www.einet.net/galaxy.html); Magellan (http://www.mckinley.com); The Whole Internet Catalog (http://nearnet.gnn.com/gnn/wic/index.html)* and, *Yahoo (http://www.yahoo.com)*, which is probably the largest directory, due to using automated programs to search for new sites, although still using human indexers to index them.[1,8,9]

Apart from general subject directories, such as the above mentioned, there are two other types of directories: specialised subject directories and clearinghouses. Specialised subject directories, as their name indicates, specialise in specific areas and provide access to the most important sites and resources in those areas. There are specialised subject guides in almost all subject areas, an example being *The Internet Movie Database (http://us.imdb.com)*. Other search directories, known as clearinghouses, are collections of various specialised search directories, either by including the specialised search directory on their own web sites or by providing a link to the Web sites of these specialised directories. Examples[10] include *Argus Clearinghouse (http://www.clearinghouse.net)* and *WWW Virtual library (http://www.w3. org/hypertext/DataSources/bySubject/overview.html)*.

SEARCH ENGINES

Search engines, rather than searching documents through an index, are based on allowing users to enter keywords that are matched against a database. Unlike subject directories, which use human indexers to build their indexes, search engines use software programs which create automatically their own databases which contain lists of Web pages. Search engines are composed of three different parts: a program called spider (or robot or crawler), a database with an index, and search software.[11-15] Spiders wander through the Web, crawling from site to site, following links between pages. Different search engines use different types of spiders. Some visit every possible site they identify, others are based on more selective principles and visit only the most popular sites. The first type of spider finds a huge volume of information in a short space of time, the latter type generates a smaller number of pages, with perhaps more relevant results. Every page found by a spider is stored in a database, and an index of its contents is built by extracting automatically words from the Web pages and sorting them alphabetically, effectively producing an inverted file. The index is, therefore, a list of each word found (except stop words) plus a set of pointers to that word's locations in the database.

Again, different search engines will follow different principles. Some will index every single word on every Web page the spider found (excluding stop words), other search engines index only the title and top level phrases of a Web site. The third element of the search engine is the search software, which is a program which compares search queries keyed in by people (for example, Search: 'marketing companies') with the index, finds matches, and ranks them in order of relevance. The criteria for judging relevance will vary according to the search engine.[16]

The different approaches which search engines use in crawling the Web, finding new pages, and indexing them will produce totally different results. This is why when searching the same topic in different search engines, there can be very striking differences in the results. Also, because of the way they operate, search engines are more oriented to find larger volumes of information and more specific information than subject directories. This is because they are based on searching entire web pages with automatic indexing of the exact words on pages, whereas subject directories only search the top levels of a site and index it with pre-defined index terms

Examples of search engines include: AltaVista (http://altavista.digital. com/); Excite (http://www.excite.com/); HotBot (http://www.hotbot. com/); Infoseek (http://www.infoseek.com/); and Lycos (http://www. lycos.com/).

As different search engines have different strengths, new search tools have been created more recently, which allow people to search simultaneously the databases of different search engines, while using one single interface. These tools are called multi-threaded search engines and although they usually do not have all the search flexibility of individual search engines, they are very fast and can search through vast amounts of information. Examples of multi-threaded search engines include: Dogpile (http://www.dogpile.com) and Metacrawler (http://www.metacrawler.com).

WORD AND CONCEPT INDEXING
AND THE WORLD WIDE WEB

Indexing systems have often been characterised as reflections of the way the human mind organises and uses knowledge. According to Anderson,[17] *"Indexing systems represent attempts to extend the organising capabilities of the human mind to [. . .] artificial (humanly devised) information storage and communication systems [i.e., writ-*

ten, sound and visual documents, transmitted by post, radio, tv, electronic networks and other communication systems]. Indexing systems turn storage and communication systems into information retrieval systems analogous, on widely varying degrees, to the human information retrieval system of the mind."

The different approaches used by subject directories and search engines in terms of indexing are not new. Subject directories use a conceptual approach, which people have been using over centuries and is at the basis of the classification schemes used in many fields (from library classifications, such as Dewey, to taxonomic classifications in biology). Search engines use more recent methods, based on the automatic extraction of words into an index, developed and adopted since the first text retrieval software applications in the 1960s and materialised in text retrieval systems based on inverted files. There are, therefore, two main types of methods for indexing or searching for documents on the World Wide Web–word based and concept based.

Word based methods concern the automatic input of words which are recorded in the documents to be described, without any further input or consideration of the exact meaning of each of the terms extracted from the source document. These words will be then used to describe the document. This method is computer based and the words are extracted regardless of their meaning. It is the fastest and more economic approach and is increasingly used. The search engines on the WWW work through automatic word indexing of Web sites.[18] Automatic indexing systems very frequently include statistical devices to assign weights to each term, and therefore determine by frequency of occurrence the most important terms in the document. It is then possible to select for representation only those most frequently occurring terms.

Concept based methods, contrary to word based methods, require the identification of the concepts which are represented by the terms used in the documents, rather than just extracting the terms used in the document. Concept based methods use concepts identified in the document by a human indexer who then selects which are the most appropriate to represent the document. As stressed by Buchanan,[19] *"concepts are ideas of things, to be distinguished from names of things."* Because of this, the index terms used to represent the document may often be different than the terms actually used in the document, as the same concept may be expressed through different terms. The creation of concepts in subject indexing is analogous to the creation of concepts in the mind, as it is based on the association of representations of objects, ideas, processes, and other entities with related data which pre-exists in the mind.[17,20]

Concept based methods require the intervention of the human mind and imply the analysis of the concepts present in the text and the choice of terms best representing a document. This method of representation is focused on the meaning of terms. It introduces an element of interpretation and is more time consuming and less economic than the previous method. Search directories in the WWW have a concept based organisation and use human indexing of the different Web sites. Concept based indexes are often structured in order to represent the relationships between the different concepts, either through the use of references (for example, Documents *See also* Reports) or by grouping related subjects together (as for example, Religion, Buddhism, Christianity, Hinduism, Islamism, Judaism). Note that the optimal order for the distinctive religions in this example need not be alphabetical.

Word indexing is fast and economic but does not consider the meaning of words. Systems which are word indexed therefore cannot distinguish between words which are spelt the same way but mean something different (a *hard exam* and a *computer hard disk,* for example). Also, different words referring to the same concept (*heart attack* and *cardiac arrest*) cannot be retrieved unless you key in every word form (if entered the query '*heart diseases,*' you would not retrieve a document which had used the expression '*cardiac diseases*' instead).

Concept based indexing used by subject directories is done by humans and is not based on extracting words from the text. It is based on identifying the meaning of words in the context where they are used and choosing one keyword or expression for each concept. These keywords or expressions will form the subject index of subject directories. Some search engines (Excite, Euroferret) try to simulate the way humans identify concepts, by making use of very sophisticated computer programs based on statistical and probabilistic calculations and/or on artificial intelligence.[15, 21-22] These programs analyse the co-occurrence of different words which relate to the same subject in order to determine what subject(s) the document is about–for example, the word *hard*

- associated with other words like *surface, stone, disk* would refer to the physical property of an object being solid
- associated with words like *exam, text, experience,* would refer to the degree of difficulty involved in certain situations
- associated with words like *person, man, woman,* would refer to personal characteristics such as unfriendliness or severity.

USING FACET ANALYSIS TO SEARCH AND ORGANIZE WWW RESOURCES

In the context of the accelerating changes in the information environment with first the IT and then the Internet revolutions, it is easy to overlook the relevance of classic techniques such as facet analysis.[23] The LIS professions, which have their intellectual and conceptual foundations in originally non-IT applications of information management, should recall that the techniques of knowledge organization which were developed in the context of manual systems and hard copy information sources are not restricted in their application to the historical source of their development. The use of facet analysis in the creation of thesauri for online databases demonstrates fresh applications. However, the development of the WWW and the proliferation of WWW information sources has taken place largely outside the sphere of LIS professions or practice. This is not to say that such professions and practices could not serve to enhance the development of the WWW, as already demonstrated by the subject directory approach, through examples such as the WWW Virtual Library. It can be argued that an information source of such size and complexity as the WWW has more to gain from the application of LIS knowledge than have small special collections.

An example of the application of facet analysis to hypertext design, and therefore to the data structure of the Internet and WWW, is Duncan's application of the principles of facet analysis to guide the creation of a knowledge structure for a hypertext database.[24-26] She applied the technique in a number of related studies including the creation of knowledge structures for hypertext databases,[24] for structuring knowledge bases for designers of learning materials[25] and for the generation of a concept map thesaurus as a hypertext interface.[26] Duncan applied facet analysis to derive an underlying model data structure transferable across subject domains. The generic facet labels would have different instantiations in different subject areas.

Duncan provides examples[27] of what the label facet descriptors might be in a 'hard skills' area such as catering compared to a 'soft skills' area such as counselling.

Generic Labels	Catering Labels	Counselling Labels
Parts	Ingredients	Attitudes
Processes	Processes	Processes
Procedures	Recipes	Procedures
Agents	Equipment	People
Properties	Characteristics	Situations
Products		

Duncan[27] suggested that facet labels could be used in connection with their relationships to generate a form of 'grammar' for the subject area. The structure of facets and relationships would be employed to generate 'sentence' templates where terms from a facet would be combined with terms from the same or other facets in a kind of reasoning system as the following example illustrates–

{Agents} <causing> {Processes}

Basis of machine 'grammar' based on recognition of facet types

Duncan also suggested that this machine 'grammar' approach could be further enriched by the creation of templates and associated icons for the different facet types. Duncan explored these ideas in more depth in relation to the structuring of learning materials for designers of learning materials. In this study,[25] Duncan explored three different approaches to knowledge elicitation and representation: (1) the concept map or concept network approach; (2) facet analysis; and (3) links and link types. In the first option subject experts generated links between concept statements as a way of expressing their knowledge about the subject area. The statements could be simple such as [probing] {is a} [communication skill] or take more complex forms such as [clients] {may want} [counsellors] {to take} [responsibility] {for} [problems].[28] These concepts and their relationships were then displayed graphically using the NoteCards system.

The use of the concept map network structure was successful in some respects in that the subject experts were able to represent knowledge expressed in natural language in the concept network map and were also able to identify inconsistencies or inadequacies in the concept network. However, problems were experienced in relation to the extent to which complex or qualified statements could be represented in the concept map network and in ambiguity of interpretation for both machine and users.

In order to reduce this ambiguity Duncan employed facet analysis to differentiate between different types of concept. She used the general facet labels Product, Part, Process, Procedure, Agent, and Property to label the NoteCards domain card types with the hypertext authors or designers re-labelling these with labels relevant to their subject area. In a social skills context these might be–'Outcomes–Details of Situations–Situations–Interviews–People–Characteristics' while in a catering context they might be 'Products–Constituents–Processes–Recipes–Ingredients–Characteristics.'[29] This use of facet analysis simplifies the process of recognition of concepts and their relationships both for the machine and the user because the display can be restricted to one facet type. However, the use of facet labels still had limitations in for knowledge representation and understanding. Duncan then combined the facet approach to knowledge elicitation and representation with the generation of a typology of links. Seven link categories were used experimentally: being; showing; causing; using; having; including and similarity. The resulting 'experimental model or cognitive tool kit'[30] had three elements–

a. a network of nodes and links where nodes are labels for concepts and links are labels for relationships
b. a set of standard card-types with templates
c. a set of standard link types.

Another interesting feature of Duncan's work has been experimentation with different ways of displaying the database structure, and, in particular with the use of thesaurus techniques to generate concept maps as knowledge based hypertext interfaces to bibliographic databases.[26] Duncan's earlier studies were on the display of citation information, on the display of hierarchic relations between concepts from educational broadcasts, and the kinds of relations elicited from children between given concepts. The first of these projects had demonstrated that the users did not perceive the need or educational value of a thesaurus, saw it as little more than a finding list for words and did not readily understand the hierarchic broader term narrower term relationships which structured the thesaurus. The last point was explored further in an experiment with a sample of 150 children between the ages of 7 and 12 designed to elicit the kind of relationships on the subject of the environment which were naturally understood by children at that age. This led to the identification[31] of 13 different kinds of relationship which were then used instead of the conventional broader term, narrower term and related term relations in the thesaurus display. The 13 relationships were:

- live(s) in/on
- is/are found in/on
- something you do with
- is/are made up of
- is/are the same kind of thing
- is/are under
- need(s)
- help(s)
- cause(s)/make(s)
- use(s)
- is/are related to
- is/are part of
- has/have an effect on

The results of these experiments persuaded Duncan of the value of graphical interfaces for displaying the kind of information contained in a conventional thesaurus, and of the utility of incorporating user defined relationships in the database and display, and not to rely on the conventional broader term, narrower term and related term relationships of a traditional thesaurus. Duncan suggested that a thesaurus of user defined relationships displayed in a graphical format presented the opportunity for developing a form of conceptual map of the subject domain. The user could then explore this map, or use it as a heuristic device for learning or understanding.

Duncan's work is a model of the application of the direct application of facet analysis to hypertext design. At a conceptual level her use of facet analysis reinforces Ingwersen and Wormell's [32] argument of the continuing relevance of Ranganathan's work for the development of information retrieval systems. There are also interesting parallels between the thinking which underpins facet analysis and the semantic model of human memory structures. The work of Vickery[33] and Lindsay and Norman[34] can be seen as representing ways of looking at complex subjects from different perspectives.

CONCLUSION

Ingwersen and Wormell[32] have already pointed out the continuing relevance of facet analysis for contemporary information retrieval. The intention here is to indicate the relevance of facet analysis in relation to searching and organising material on the World Wide Web. This is of relevance not only for those who design or develop Web pages but also for anyone searching the Web. One of the major sources of problems involved in searching the WWW is that in most cases *"there is no closeness at all between designer or creator (which could be anyone) and potential user (which could be anyone or everyone) . . . the more distant users are, in characteristics and information needs from the types of user conceived of and catered for by those creating or indexing a database, the more likely there are to be problems in accessing relevant information by users from that database."*[35] This is a general problem which is not necessarily resolvable by refining either the indexing or searching on the WWW. Consider the kind of material which would be considered relevant and that which would be considered outlandish in the case of an identical search on the subject of UFOs by a NASA scientist or an *X-Files* fan–assuming they were not one and the same person.

The problem of lack of proximity between searcher and source, of not knowing which item or source will be 'relevant' in a search because of the disparity between individual searchers, and the conceptual as well as physical distance between searchers and sources has been referred to as the problem of "indexing for the unknown user."[35] This problem removes the foundations of many contemporary indexing or search algorithms which have to make many such assumptions as the core of their foundations. The fact that the same search would produce disparate relevance rankings depending on whether it was undertaken by the NASA scientist or the aficionado of *The X-Files* is not present in the assumptions of contemporary information retrieval research or practice. That is not to say that such techniques do not have their place but the WWW might not be that place.

Much contemporary work in information retrieval research is a direct descendent of the Cranfield tests of indexing languages and indexing devices. The model of the retrieval interaction underlying contemporary research is that embodied in the Cranfield tests.[36] This approach in which a user with an information need comes to an information system can be described as the information retrieval model. The information system contains information, usually in the form of documents on a subject, and representations of that information. The information need of the user is expressed as a query or elicited in some form of problem statement. The terms of the query or problem statement are matched against the terms in the database of information and representations. The user is presented with those items which the system infers, either via Boolean logic or probabilistic calculation, most closely match the user's query or problem statement. These items may be displayed to the user unranked or ranked in terms of the systems calculation of probability of relevance. In relevance feedback systems the user's relevance judgements may be used to further search or re-rank the information or representations. The performance of the system is judged on its ability to identify relevant items (recall) and hold back irrelevant ones (precision).

Classically this model has been criticised for a number of its assumptions:

- that the user is able to formulate his need in a well formulated request
- that the relevance judgement is fixed and not dynamic in the course of the retrieval interaction
- that the relevance evaluation is binary
- that the user can recognise an information need rather than being in an uncertain or anomalous state of knowledge, etc.

Some of these criticisms have been addressed in some form or another in the literature and in empirical studies. Other assumptions which are made in the model but which have not received so much attention are:

- that the information on the database is in some sense 'about' the subject the user is interested in
- that the user can be treated somewhat homogeneously.

These assumptions were fundamental to the Cranfield tests. There the subject was aerodynamics and the user a scientist. These assumptions arose naturally from the test environment. In that sense, information retrieval research has its intellectual origins in special librarianship. The information systems which were the archetypes for contemporary information retrieval research were those which specialised in particular subjects, and the users were the scientists specialising in the area of the subject. These assumptions have not been seen as problematic for contemporary information retrieval research because of two factors:

- the databases, either in practice or in the form of test collections, have usually been quite constrained in terms of their subject matter
- the user groups have also usually been quite restricted or constrained in terms of the assumptions made about them in terms of their ability to provide queries or problem statements and their ability to make relevance judgements.

However, the development and widespread availability of globally distributed information systems to widely diffuse and disparate groups of users via the Internet and World Wide Web makes the relationship between the information retrieval model and behavioural reality increasingly tenuous. This is due to the breakdown in the connection between the database or Website designer and the searcher.

Facet analysis cannot solve the problem of indexing for the unknown user. However, because it adopts an *a posteriori* not *a priori* approach to classification, that is the classification is derived inductively from the concepts or terms used in the subject field, it can alleviate some problems in searching the WWW by being applied to using subject directories or search engines. In that respect, facet analysis merges together word and concept based approaches, in that the concept terms in the facets are selected on the basis of literary warrant. Therefore facet analysis can assist the developer or searcher to index or search the WWW in a reasonably effective and efficient way. It cannot eliminate the problem of indexing for the unknown user but it can ameliorate it by providing a means of assisting the search process and organizing the search results.

In terms of searching, facet analysis can be used to suggest, arrange, and organize the terms which would be used in a WWW search. The initial selection of terms for the facet analysis can proceed in a conventional manner by drawing on reference works, but alternatively a broad search on the WWW itself is likely to generate a reasonable set of terms for a facet analysis. The resulting classification should therefore provide a convenient form of organization of search terms for a subject field. It can also be employed to organize WWW resources, not as a whole, but in relation to organizing the results of WWW searches and in relation to Web page indexing. The terms of the facet classification can be used in the search as well as to organize the search page. The general index search page or pages can also be made 'live' by the provision of links to sites judged relevant from the search itself. These sites can be linked to the terms of the classification on the screen. This makes the facet display live. In subsequent searches this would enable the searcher to go straight from the chosen search terms to the sites identified or considered as relevant from previous searches. This feature has, in fact, been successfully implemented experimentally in prototype facet search structures by students on the MSc in Information Management at the Faculty of Engineering, University of Porto, Portugal.

Maximising the matching process to optimise or refine the identification of 'relevant' documents cannot work in the WWW environment in the same way as it might in the test collection environment, due to lack of control over the creation of WWW material and general lack of proximity between searcher and sources. However, facet analysis can be used to optimise the information retrieval interaction by taking into account both the objective characteristics of the WWW materials and the subjective needs of the searcher. It can thus assist in managing the information retrieval interaction for optimal result. Other information retrieval techniques may not do this because of the very assumptions made about the information retrieval interaction in their development. By introducing an element of judgement or knowledge organisation attuned to the searcher as well as to the terms of the subject field, the general philosophy underlying facet analysis is more attuned to information retrieval interaction in the WWW environment.

REFERENCES

1. J. H. Ellsworth, and M.V. Ellsworth, *The new Internet business book.* (New York: J. Wiley and Sons, 1996).

2. M. Handley and J. Cowcroft, *The World Wide Web beneath the surf.* (London: UCL Press, 1995).

3. T. H. Nelson, *Computer lib.*, (Chicago: Nelson, 1974).

4. T. H. Nelson, "Replacing the printed word: A complete literary system", in: S. H. Lavington, ed. *Information processing 80*, (New York: North Holland, 1980). p.1013-1023.

5. T. H. Nelson, *Literary machines*, (Swathmore: Nelson, 1981).

6. T. H. Nelson, "The tyranny of the file: A bold new approach to storing data could sweep away many difficulties users face", *Datamation* 32, (1986): 83-84, 86.

7. T. H. Nelson, "Managing immense storage", *Byte* 13, (1988): 225-238.

8. P. Gilster, *Finding it on the Internet: the Internet navigator's guide to search tools and techniques* (New York: John Wiley and Sons, 1996).

9. G. Venditto, "Cybercritic services rate Web sites. Which is best? IW Labs rates the raters." *Internet World* Jan. 1997. <http://www.internetworld.com/print/monthly/199701/wlabs.html> (1997).

10. R. Tyner, *Sink or swim: Internet search tools and techniques* <http://www.sci.ouc.bc.ca/libr/connect96/search.htm#search.> (1997).

11. D. Sullivan, *Search engines features chart.* <http://searchenginewatch.internet.com./webmasters/features.html> (1998).

12. D. Sullivan, *How search engines rank Web pages.* <http://searchenginewatch.internet.com/webmasters/rank.html> (1998).

13. D. Sullivan, *How search engines work.* <http://searchenginewatch.internet.com/webmasters/work.html> (1998).

14. D. Sullivan, *The major search engines.* <http://searchenginewatch.internet.com/facts/major.html> (1998).

15. D. Haskin, *The right search engine: IW labs test.* <http://www.internetworld.com/print/monthly/1997/09/report.html> (1997).

16. Binghamton University Libraries, *Comparing search engines.* <http://library.lib.binghamton.edu/webdocs/search-engine-comparison.html> (1998).

17. J.D. Anderson, "Indexing systems: extensions of the mind's organizing power", in: *Information and behaviour*. B.D. Ruben, ed. (New Brunswick: Transaction Books, 1985), 287-323, p.287-288.

18. B. C. O'Connor, *Explorations in indexing and abstracting: Pointing, virtue and power.* (Englewood: Libraries Unlimited 1996).

19. B. Buchanan, *Theory of library classification.* (London: Clive Bingley, 1979). p. 12.

20. A.C. Foskett, *The subject approach to information.* (London: Library Association, 1996).

21. D. Ellis, N. Ford, and J. Furner, "In search of the unknown user: Indexing, hypertext and the World Wide Web." *Journal of Documentation*, 54 (1998): 28-47.

22. L. Barlow, *The Spider's aprentice: how to use Web search engines.* <http://www.monash.com/spidap4.html> (1997).

23. S. R. Ranganathan, *Prolegomena to Library Classification.* (London: The Library Association, 1937).

24. E. B. Duncan, "A faceted approach to hypertext", in: R. McAleese, ed. *Hypertext: Theory into practice*, (London: Intellect Limited, 1989): 157-163.

25. E. B. Duncan, "Structuring knowledge bases for designers of learning materials", *Hypermedia* 1 (1989): 20-32.

26. E. B. Duncan, "A concept map thesaurus as a knowledge-based hypertext interface to a bibliographic database", *Informatics 10: Prospects for Intelligent Retrieval*, (London: Aslib, 1990): 43-52.

27. as 24, p.160-161.

28. as 25, p.23.

29. as 25, p.28.

30. as 25, p.32.

31. as 26, p.46.

32. P. Ingwersen and I. Wormell, "Ranganathan in the perspective of advanced information retrieval" *Libri 42*(1992):184-201.

33. B. C. Vickery, "Knowledge representation: a brief review", *Journal of Documentation* 42 (1986): 145-159.

34. P. H. Lindsay, and D. A. Norman,. *Human information processing*, 2nd ed. (New York: Academic Press, 1977).

35. as 21. p.44.

36. D. Ellis, *Progress and problems in information retrieval* (London: Library Association Publishing, 1996).

Subject Trees on the Internet: A New Rôle for Bibliographic Classification?

Alan Wheatley

SUMMARY. Internet information retrieval is largely the preserve of search engines and the even more popular subject trees. Subject trees have adapted principles of conventional bibliographic classification for structuring hierarchic browsing interfaces, thus providing easily used pathways to their selected resources. This combination of browsing and selectivity is especially valuable to untrained users. For the foreseeable future, it appears that subject trees will remain the Internet's only practicable use of classificatory methods for information retrieval. *[Article copies available for a fee from The Haworth Document Delivery Service: 1-800-342-9678. E-mail address: getinfo@haworthpressinc.com <Website: http://www.haworthpressinc.com>]*

KEYWORDS. Classification, indexing, information retrieval, Internet, Internet information retrieval, subject trees, gateways, subject gateways, Excite, Britannica, e-BLAST, Infoseek, GO Network, Look-Smart, Lycos Top 5%, Yahoo

INTRODUCTION

Bibliographic classification, as seen in the Dewey Decimal and Library of Congress Classification schemes, can be broadly defined as:

Alan Wheatley is Lecturer in the Department of Information and Library Studies, University of Wales, Llanbadarn Fawr, Aberystwyth, Ceredigion SY23 3AS, United Kingdom (alw@aber.ac.uk).

[Haworth co-indexing entry note]: "Subject Trees on the Internet: A New Rôle for Bibliographic Classification?" Wheatley, Alan. Co-published simultaneously in *Journal of Internet Cataloging* (The Haworth Information Press, an imprint of The Haworth Press, Inc.) Vol. 2, No. 3/4, 2000, pp. 115-141; and: *Internet Searching and Indexing: The Subject Approach* (ed: Alan R. Thomas, and James R. Shearer) The Haworth Information Press, an imprint of The Haworth Press, Inc., 2000, pp. 115-141. Single or multiple copies of this article are available for a fee from The Haworth Document Delivery Service [1-800-342-9678, 9:00 a.m. - 5:00 p.m. (EST). E-mail address: getinfo@haworthpressinc.com].

115

a means of organising resources or surrogates into browsable, hierarchically related, groups, each group comprising a set of items having more in common with each other than with items in other groups, and each item having some means of readily determining its relative location.

Intentionally, this is a broad definition, not mentioning accessories such as notation (for expressing and "mechanising" classified order) and indexes (for convenient formal retrieval), or the environment of use (such as a public library). Implicitly, it includes some form of schedule in which classes are named with any instructions needed by classifiers. With these caveats, I'm perfectly happy to see classified document collections in libraries and the pages of subject trees such as Yahoo occupying the same conceptual space, where item collocations are essentially subject based, and determined by similarities of the classified items. For the purposes of this text, subject trees are understood to be:

> Internet based, hierarchically organised, electronic collections of (subject) headings and item descriptions providing browsable access to information materials (usually Internet materials). The materials are normally selected, described and indexed by editors with relevant subject or library and information expertise (Figure 1).

Classification has been important for library-based information retrieval for so long that its particular properties and suitabilities have almost been forgotten. Current librarianship textbooks generally neglect today's dominant application of classification–to provide browsable sequences of documents or document entries for direct retrieval by end users. Browsable classified document collections and [classified] Internet subject trees such as Yahoo and gateways are now the most important applications of classificatory principles. Gateways also need a definition to clarify their relationship with subject trees. Gateways are:

> generally similar to the major subject trees, with selective acquisition, description and organisation of resources into browsable hierarchies by skilled human editors, but are usually highly subject specialised in content and employ much shallower hierarchies.

FIGURE 1. Yahoo is the classical subject tree. Here, six of its hierarchic levels are represented in a browsing search for information on "horse sports." The searcher has been tempted by a top level heading for sports, and has followed the hierarchic path: *Recreation & Sports > Sports > [Horse Racing] > Equestrian* to some of Yahoo's selected Web sites.

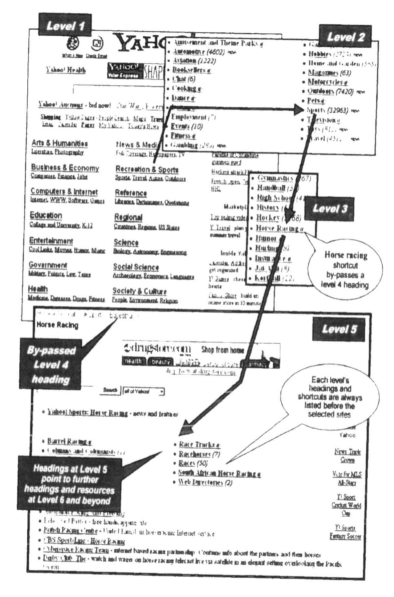

To avoid misunderstanding, the definition of browsing adopted here is an:

> activity allowing searchers to explore hierarchically organised sets of information materials and to simply broaden and narrow their search by moving up and down the hierarchies. This activity takes place when shelf browsing, and when exploring a classified file of index entries or a subject tree. No formal, verbal, search statement is required.

This text examines aspects of Internet subject trees and gateways, because they appear uniquely able to provide a painless information retrieval tool for large collections of Internet resources.

If pressed into a definition of the *Internet* I'm inclined to be even less specific because a pragmatic (i.e., useful) non-technical definition is likely to become rapidly obsolete, and to grow into an obstacle to progress. For the purposes of this text and its information retrieval context I offer:

> a system of networks offering resources of information and services, and providing facilities to store, interrogate, and deliver these resources to the public.

Obviously, private networks using Internet techniques for their information organisation, delivery, etc., share much with this definition, but their privacy often allows them luxuries, such as formal user training, that are unthinkable for the world wide public Internet.

In the library and information context, discussions centred on the words *classification* and *Internet* beg a number of uncomfortable questions that can be summarised as:

- How broadly should classification be defined?
- What is the library approach to classification on the Internet, or, the dreadful state of OPACs!
- What kinds of classification are currently used in classifying Internet resources?
- What kind of classification do subject trees and gateways use?
- What kinds of material, and what elements of the material, are classified?
- Who performs the classification?

- What are the classifier's aims when classifying material for subject trees?
- Who is using Internet subject trees?
- How and why do users benefit from classification and subject trees?
- How do these users employ classification and subject trees?
- Can a study of these questions help to discover the information retrieval properties of a good subject tree?

Answers to these questions are considered below.

THE QUESTIONS AND THEIR IMPLICATIONS

There are many answers to the questions above, but they can all be conveniently grouped into two schools of thought. The formal, library oriented school tends to see classification in terms of the bibliographic approach and OPACs, and stresses a long term view of resource organisation arising from the need to care for traditional paper-based resources. The successes of this approach are demonstrated in the achievements of the major tools, Dewey Decimal Classification and Library of Congress Classification, now honed by a century or more of invention and compromise. Despite their well-known imperfections, these systems have supported widely different users and given them simple, though not comprehensive, access to the smallest and largest collections in the public and academic library worlds. This school's thinking is necessarily constrained by the physical nature of library resources, and by the need to provide simultaneous access to both volatile materials and those with many years of useful life.

For a century or more, the established view of the information retrieval community in Europe was that classified document sequences, with supporting alphabetical indexes to their classmarks, were the most effective retrieval tools for large library collections. Such was the stifling power of the official view that the classified approach was also popular with the producers of printed subject indexes, and generations of librarians professed themselves mystified at catalogue users' reluctance to wade painfully through the multiple stages of classified retrieval. Though it was never formally revoked, this classification centred view was profoundly questioned by the Cranfield experiments,[1,2] and began fading towards insignificance in the 1970s. The rise of OPACs in the 1980s, with their singularly incompetent handling of classified information (see below), delivered a coup de grâce to formal classified retrieval methods in the library.

In contrast to this "official" conception of classification is the users' countermanding view. This embraces a far more informal school of thought on classification developed in the flexible world of Internet and WWW indexing, where subject trees such as Yahoo[3] and Excite[4] began to successfully apply a looser form of classification to substantial collections of electronic documents. Unconstrained by the physical demands of shelf arrangement and permanent collections of labelled items, they cheerfully ignored the special tools and tricks developed for bibliographic classification schemes, such as academically defined main classes, austere tables of standard subdivisions, literary warrant, notation, etc., and concentrated upon simplicity of use. This "Internet school" sees classification as a simple hierarchic interpretation of users' current needs rather than an academic view of permanent knowledge, and exploits the rapid turnover of electronic resources in justifying a more dynamic and volatile approach to representing knowledge. Thus today's minor subheading may become tomorrow's major class, and a loose agglomeration of topics such as "home" can be as important as an established academic entity such as "politics." Equally important, because there is no necessity for shelf location, there is no need to designate one view of an item as more important than all others. In the world of virtual resources, an item can have as many virtual locations as its users might need.

I carry a torch for neither of these approaches: they serve different users and different needs. They are the productions of different circumstances, and they are remarkably complementary in their strengths and weaknesses. In the questions below I want to draw your attention, positively, to a developing strong relationship between bibliographic and bibliothecal classification as it has been performed in the past, and classification as it is now being applied by the Internet subject trees and gateways.

HOW BROADLY SHOULD CLASSIFICATION BE DEFINED?

Classification is a tool that libraries have used very effectively for the past century and half to organise their materials into browsable collections. In all this time, the basic principle of organisation has remained the obvious one of hierarchic grouping–the only principle compatible with low-cost operation, end-user access, and minimal user training. The recent introductions of electronic materials, the Internet, and virtual libraries have done nothing to undermine that crucial principle. In fact it has become more important: low operating costs, and successful access by virtually untrained users are the Internet's dominating imperatives.

Nineteenth century libraries, modern supermarkets, and Internet information providers are all driven by the power of that second imperative, which could also be stated as the economic necessity of operating self-service systems whilst avoiding the cost and difficulties of significant user training. In all these cases the operators have arrived at similar solutions to their problems. They have built controlled vocabulary retrieval systems (respectively employing hierarchic bibliographical classification, generalised shelf labels, and hierarchically organised descriptive subject headings) that sacrifice precision retrieval methods in favour of simple browsing operation.

So, an answer to the question of how broadly classification should be defined must encompass all methods of exploiting browsable hierarchies. This capacious, and somewhat gauche, response has a particularly striking and very significant side effect–it excludes most OPACs, and so points an accusing finger at these eminent devices. The accusing finger is there because most OPACs are not hierarchically browsable, and they can be searched only as alphabetical devices (further discussion below). I do not believe it is honest to regard such OPACs as representatives of the classified approach to retrieval.

WHAT IS THE LIBRARY APPROACH TO CLASSIFICATION ON THE INTERNET, OR, THE DREADFUL STATE OF OPACS!

With varying imagination and success, libraries have applied full-scale bibliographic classification to collections of paper and electronic resources, and have made the results available via the Internet. The success of this has ranged from the revelatory (sadly rare) to the appalling (regrettably frequent), and has depended largely on the degree to which the potentials of electronic access methods have been recognised. At the nadir of this approach is the typical library OPAC's classified search option. If you doubt the truly abysmal depth of information retrieval malpractice that has produced these sorry OPACs, use one for yourself, now. You'll probably discover that the information contained in its classmarks is searchable only by exact matching of classmarks in the search statement with *complete* classmarks in the index, and that there is none of the easy broadening and narrowing that a hierarchic classified search could and should extend to users. After you have examined the OPAC, compare its clumsy inflexibility with the comfortable flexibility of browsing Yahoo–which also presents hierarchically organised resources.

Bibliographic classifiers ideally provide their catalogues with powerfully hierarchic classmarks that express the multiple inter-relationships of a complex document's subjects, and represent them compactly in a classmark of a dozen or so exquisitely controlled characters. Though OPACs readily absorb these few characters, and will display them on demand, most OPAC search software has little understanding of the wisdom built into these characters, and can do little more than crudely match a search string with a classmark. Hierarchy is normally ignored, and common groups of characters in classmarks cannot be identified except through generic truncation facilities. The loss of information goes further. Any cross references and scope notes in the classification scheme's schedule and index, that might have identified related classes, will be entirely unknown to the OPAC. In a classic circular justification, the information is never loaded, because the search software has no facility for understanding it, and the understanding is not provided because there is no information to use with it.

All these points contribute powerfully to a typical OPAC's dreadfully limited response to "classified" searches: it can answer only queries for which the searcher already knows the most difficult part of the answer–the full classmark. The user who wants allied classes is not satisfied by this, nor is the user who wants broader classes, and nor is the user who wants occurrences of the same concept within other classes. Furthermore, the user who doesn't know the classmark cannot find it, and none of these users is offered a helpful means of browsing proximate entries. Comprehensive failure, brought about by technical limitations and professional ignorance, is the only possible description of this sad state. Since OPACs were created, a century of earlier developments in classification has been casually smothered. Initially, and justifiably, the technical capabilities of the machines and their software were responsible, but over the last decade the blame has passed to vendors who haven't understood classification, and to librarians who have been feebly content with the limited OPAC software they purchased. In the future marketplace, perhaps interoperability standards, such as Z59.50, will persuade OPAC buyers to take their library management software from one vendor and their OPAC's user interface from another, separating searching interface developments from the core database management facilities.

There have been some encouraging developments, so it would be wrong to leave the impression that using classificatory principles for OPAC searching is a lost cause. For example, search trees have been introduced to help users make the best use of the information they bring to the catalogue;[5] a mainstream vendors catalogue for children exploits hierarchic principles and icons to promote a simpler browsing style of retrieval;[6] and Borgman has campaigned for and experimented with imaginative approaches to OPAC searching for children.[7] This kind of innovation and progress is welcome: libraries were among the first institutions to put computerised information retrieval into the hands of ordinary people, and it is sad that progress since then has been very limited.

The library approach to retrieval is associated with two strengths: an expectation of the permanence of the resources they index, and a curatorial sense of responsibility for the long-term value of these resources. However, this permanence is reflected in the comparative inertia of bibliographical classification systems, forming a serious handicap to the free development of their access tools. Thus libraries have so far contributed little to a synergy of classification and Internet resources. We must look elsewhere for this.

WHAT KINDS OF CLASSIFICATION ARE CURRENTLY USED IN CLASSIFYING INTERNET RESOURCES?

This is the fundamental question about the uses of classification on the Internet, for its answer determines the limits within which all the remaining questions must be examined. Unsurprisingly, this fundamental question's answer has several parts–none of them owing a debt of any importance to standard OPACs.

A very comprehensive report[8] showed that traditional library classification is modestly represented on the Internet. A dozen or more Web sites display respectable collections of general or specialised materials, hierarchically arranged by Dewey Decimal Classification or Library of Congress Classification, or by less well-known schemes, such as those of the US National Library of Medicine, and the Engineering Information Classification Codes. The CyberStacks site[9] has information on some of the Internet's less conventional uses of classification.

Though there are sufficient examples of library classification schemes applied to Internet materials to demonstrate the technical capabilities of this approach, few of the examples are large scale catalogues with most of the classification's niches occupied, and these examples are not sufficient to provide convincing evidence of its practicality. The Internet world's verdict on the value of the library classification tradition can be seen in these statistics. Despite libraries' decades-long head start in acquiring materials and the techniques of solving information retrieval problems, the tradition has fallen by the Internet wayside. After half a decade of muted World Wide Web activity, the traditional library classification approach can muster few effective sites, and most of them present a fairly static inventory of just a few thousand documents, and attract few users each day. Contrast this with the two largest Internet subject trees. In five years Yahoo, and more recently LookSmart,[10] have grown from nothing until they now index well over half a million Internet documents between them, and are used millions of times each day. The contrasts in size and usage say all that need be said about the probable futures of the libraries' formal classificatory approach and the subject trees' informal hierarchies.

Figuratively, the users have already voted with their feet. In the strongest possible terms, they have said they want their classified Internet resources presented via easily browsable informal verbal hierarchies, and not in the form of a traditional library classification.

WHAT KIND OF CLASSIFICATION DO SUBJECT TREES AND GATEWAYS USE?

Starting from a computer oriented perspective, and with neither the benefits nor the blinkers of bibliographic classification, the developers of subject trees transformed their early lists of Internet resources into hierarchically organised retrieval tools that users could easily browse. They enthusiastically embraced the fundamental principles of hierarchy, demonstrated so convincingly in bibliographic classification schemes, and displayed their resources as alphabetically labelled, hierarchically nested sets of items (Yahoo, Excite, etc.). To this day, a debt to bibliographic classification and library practice can be seen in Yahoo's cross references between headings (marked by the @ symbol in Yahoo's displays). Later, the subject gateways saw the common sense of the subject tree's pragmatic approach, and simplified it for their own less elaborate needs, for example, EEVL,[11] OMNI,[12] PICK.[13]

The strengths of the subject trees' and gateways' approach are easy creation and simplicity of use. The former is especially adapted to the needs of a growing or volatile collection, and the latter to a rapidly growing pool of users unskilled in the niceties of classification. A fine example of the pursuit of simplicity and easy use can be seen at the OMNI gateway, where the alphabetical "hierarchy" of resources is only one level deep (Figure 2), and even the US National Library of Medicine's classificatory structure is presented as an alphabetical list of topics (Figure 3).

WHAT KINDS OF MATERIAL AND WHAT ELEMENTS OF THE MATERIAL ARE CLASSIFIED?

If material has identifiable subject content or user interest, it can be conveniently "classified" with the subject tree approach. Admittedly, materials such as images, audio files, and maps can be difficult to classify, but classifying them is scarcely harder than assigning verbal descriptors to them.

In the past, when classification was applied to only traditional library materials, and the results were displayed in traditional catalogues, there were powerful management pressures to impose cost and skill limits on the classifier's work. These limits were critically dependent on the value or expected life of the materials, on the cost of creating and filing new catalogue entries, on the presence of existing catalogue entries, and on the likely frequency of use of new entries and materials. Good catalogue managers were never wasteful of their human resources, and so the extent of classification and the multiplication of catalogue entries were very tightly controlled, taking appropriate notice of the expected value and life of the materials.

However, the very different management pressures of an electronic setting cause the significance of these limits to be viewed in a very different light. Creating entries for subject trees is simpler and cheaper than bibliographical classification because:

1. The vocabulary used by subject trees is briefer, simpler, and more readily modified to suit awkward cases (subject trees have no problems of entrenched library attitudes or retrospective compatibility with previous editions).
2. Classification is simpler because there is no need to identify a "primary place" as a shelf location (in a subject tree, all locations can have equal potential value).
3. The subject tree classifier does not have to create alphabetical index entries to interpret the classmarks (being numbers or other symbols, classmarks are not directly understandable by users).
4. Filing entries for subject trees is cheaper and simpler because there are only alphabetical entries to file.
5. The life expectancy of electronic materials is normally much shorter than library materials, and users seem to place a premium on new and fashionable materials, so particularly careful or exhaustive or precise classification of them is discouraged because such classification is likely to be superseded quite quickly owing to the withdrawal of the material or its replacement by something newer.

Interestingly, the electronic setting can also provide some fresh document attributes to employ in classification. Search engines already exploit some of these attributes, such as measurements of the size of electronic documents, popularity with users, image content, frequency of updating, frequency of citation, etc.,[14] and use this information when ranking search output. Metrics such as these could also be used in the organisation of classified documents to supplement present subject based arrangements. However, exploiting this extra information might require that more information be demanded from users, challenging the freedom and simplicity of browsing that users now enjoy.

Subject tree vendors try to offer something to appeal to all possible users. In addition to a wide range of conventional electronic information resources, most offer travel services, stock prices, news feeds, etc. The recent rush to acquire more users by converting plain subject trees into multi-purpose portals (best displayed at the home page for Excite's subject tree and search engine[4]) did not invent this tendency, it simply cultivated a trend that was already present. The evident success with which sites like Yahoo handle this great variety of material is

FIGURE 2. OMNI's structure is representative of the flatter and simpler configurations preferred by the subject gateways, which have more limited special resources and coverage than the general subject trees, and less need of deep hierarchies. This is OMNI's "By topic, alphabetically" option, using a simplification of the US National Library of Medicine's terms, presented as hierarchy of two levels (here, *Biology > BioNet TLP Home Page*). It provides workers from medical fields with the twin advantages of accessible hierarchy and familiar vocabulary.

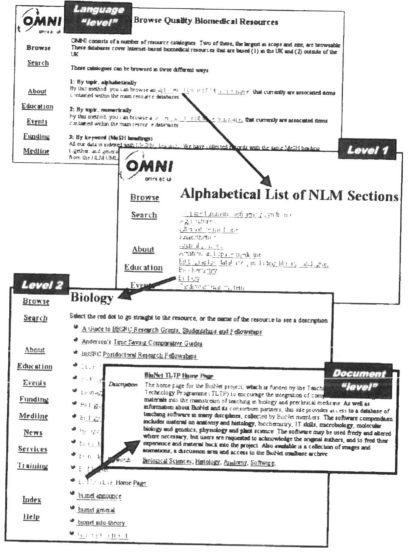

FIGURE 3. This is OMNI's "By topic, numerically" option–an apparently classified hierarchy that starts with major class marks from the US National Library of Medicine's classification scheme but then switches to more familiar alphabetical terms at the next level to preserve a shallow hierarchy (here, *QH1: Biology > Biology > BioNet TLP Home Page*). This approach provides users with a search that begins in a manner akin to shelf browsing but which soon converts into a choice from familiar alphabetical terms.

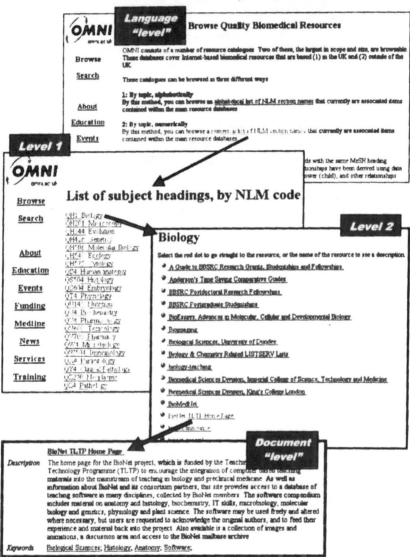

encouraging evidence of the inherent strength of the simplified classification systems used by subject trees.

Such wide ranges of user needs are very difficult to satisfy. They are beyond the scope of traditional library collections and their retrieval methods, and are likely to remain so, because public collections are normally set up only in response to closely defined long term needs. The evident success of subject trees in meeting this variety of needs is certainly worthy of note, though the extent and reliability of these successes have not been studied in significant retrieval tests.

WHO PERFORMS THE CLASSIFICATION?

In many cases, librarians from the old book-based libraries have become the classifiers of choice in the new Internet environment. Many of the subject trees frequently use their own pages to advertise for new staff, and their advertisements commonly have strong hints that applicants from the library and information workplace will be especially welcome. Over its five years of operation, Yahoo has been particularly consistent in recognising the value of library and information skills and experience for would-be Web indexers and classifiers. Their employment advertisements (a coarse phrase, "invitations" would be a gentler description) clearly recognise the value of attracting applicants with the envelope of skills needed to select, assess, summarise, organise and classify Web documents.

However, it's all too easy for librarians to bask in a warm glow of self-approval, and assume that all subject tree vendors are beneficent guardians of the old order. The newer, smaller, and hungrier subject trees are adopting a cheaper philosophy. When they invite resource creators to submit new Web pages, they commonly ask the creators to suggest appropriate subject headings and to supply 20-40 word site descriptions–coincidentally, this is the typical length of subject tree reviews (some examples of subject tree submission forms can be seen at LookSmart,[10] Yahoo,[3] and Yep.com[15]). Commercial pressures clearly make it very tempting for vendors to adopt the suggested headings as their own, and to offer the page creator's descriptions as if they were their own reviews. And, when hard-pressed subject tree vendors seem able to mount suggested pages within a day or two, it's very difficult to believe they have been able to independently view, assess, classify, and review all the pages in question.

Thus the disinterested professional indexer and classifier is being supplemented, and may even be supplanted, by the thoroughly interested creators of the resources presented by the subject trees, and there are even rumours of automated replacements for some human classification at subject trees. In the future, it is possible that objective resource selection and assessment will be the only significant human input into subject trees, and human classification of resources may fade away under the influence of economic pressures.

As a footnote to this area, it is interesting to note two possible future developments. Firstly, the classification work performed at subject trees has always been done by a staff of human indexers inserting documents into a pre-existing hierarchy. However, the OKAPI[16] project's ideas on search trees (sets of provisional search terms and strategies, automatically generated by the search software from users input and system records of previous searches and stored documents) have some interesting parallels with the conditional/hierarchic structure of subject trees. These ideas were recently investigated by Drabenstott and Weller, [5] who found search trees were about as effective in retrieval as conventional alphabetical methods. These similarities might well be exploited to limit the extensive human indexer input that subject tree production now demands. Secondly, the Open Directory Project[17,18] (jointly operated with HotBot, Lycos and Netscape) encourages users to create the Open Directory[19] subject tree by providing headings and descriptions for sites they have selected, and by maintaining entire categories of entries. At July 1999 Open Directory had indexed 750,000 Web sites, had 13,000 contributors, and was growing strongly.[20]

WHAT ARE THE CLASSIFIER'S AIMS WHEN CLASSIFYING MATERIAL FOR SUBJECT TREES?

The fact that Internet materials differ from conventional library materials is so obvious that it has to be stated very clearly to ensure it isn't overlooked. Internet materials can have volatile–even dynamic–content, can be easily superseded, and can be offered as an unlimited number of virtual copies for easier browsing. In contrast, most library materials have static content, are fairly permanent and, even when multiple copies are available, they must be stored at just one location for easier management (despite the adverse impact of this on browsing access).

These properties translate into different sets of options for the classifier. The library classifier must normally work within a framework of *permanently* located items, and must ruthlessly minimise the material's lifetime administration costs, so items can have only one expensively defined location, and the initial decision on location will usually last for the full lifetime of the item. Compare this with the greater freedoms enjoyed by the subject tree classifier. The act of classification is simpler and cheaper because of the simpler alphabetical index language. Items have virtual not physical locations, and because materials will never need to be re-shelved they can have multiple virtual locations to reflect an item's many facets. Because subject tree classification is cheaper, locations can easily be changed or their number can be increased to reflect changing user needs.

WHO IS USING THE INTERNET SUBJECT TREES?

The evidence for who is using the classified Internet subject trees is both loose and indirect. Many publicly available surveys have tried to paint pictures of the "typical" Internet user, but surveys of the users of specific commercial sites are subject to the usual commercial restrictions. General survey results have been interesting, but not surprising, and have usually suggested profiles of several classes of user. Males and females are reported to be present in increasingly balanced numbers. Wide ranges of ages and incomes are present, with the older and wealthier ends of the scales usually being better represented. It's no longer a certainty that either the information creator's or the user's first language is English. And most users have better than average educational attainment.

In trying to assemble these points into composite portraits of Internet users, the surveys concur in identifying about three categories of person. An established cadre of heavyweight users is made up of professional, managerial, and educational people who generate relatively intense business and educational traffic, but do not consciously pay for their Internet usage. At home, many of these same people are also part of a more widely defined group who pay for the Internet services that are a significant part of their recreation and lifestyle, and also part of their children's education and recreation. The third group is almost a class of remainders: the membership is so diverse it comfortably accommodates a spectrum from political analysts to social misfits, from hobbyists to professional journalists, and from athletes to the housebound. So broad is this third grouping that it clearly defies useful analysis in a short text. However, there is some common ground among all these varied groups.

In summary, Internet users tend to have higher incomes (or to spend their lower incomes in a focused manner), higher educational attainment, and to concentrate strongly on their informational, educational, and recreational needs. In short, Internet users could have almost any commercial, educational, or economic background, but they all perceive the Internet's potential for helping them meet some of their needs, and most are aware of cost and ease of use issues of Internet resources.

The expansive nature of these groupings is a reminder of a problem peculiar to the still rapidly growing Internet. Its users will always include many who are new and inexperienced, and they will always be so diverse and so scattered as to be almost permanently beyond the reach of economic effective user instruction. These novice users will usually respond most effectively to intuitive interfaces that need little or no instruction–such as hierarchically organised subject trees. Little instruction is needed because hierarchic organisation is something we all learn in childhood, when we build frameworks of knowledge, and expand our understanding by fitting new information hierarchically into contexts we already understand. Subject tree interfaces can be intuitive because vendors take care that their headings employ popular and easily understood terms, and usually represent topics from the perspective of everyday life (terminology can be appropriately technical in fields of professional and hobbyist interest).

HOW AND WHY DO USERS BENEFIT FROM CLASSIFICATION AND SUBJECT TREES?

Having said something about the Internet's users, and why they use the Internet, it's possible to draw some conclusions about their interactions with classified information materials. Though users may be relatively skilled and educated, this will not always be the case. They will often be like me, or you, or the user next door: fairly skilled and knowledgeable about some points, but unskilled and quite ignorant about others. Sometimes they will be able to apply their knowledge to a classified resource list, and will use it effectively, with intelligence and discrimination–just like you or me. But sometimes they will be faced with a strange resource and a strange topic, and they will have no alternative but to suck it and see–just like you or me!

At moments like these, when desperation looms grimly above the search, the hierarchic organisation of a classified list produces its greatest benefits for unskilled or unknowing users. A hierarchic system's provisions allow users to painlessly choose a likely top-level heading, and to progressively drill down through the hierarchy, whilst often receiving the benefits of relevance feedback to modify their search. These constitute search aids far beyond the hopes of any other system's users. It is certainly true that information retrieval thesauri offer hierarchic organisation as well as alphabetical access, but the complexity of their system of BT (Broader Term) and NT (Narrower Term) references fails the test of simplicity for novice users.

Hierarchic properties can be expressed symbolically in the notation of a classification scheme, or more informally in the subordinated ranks of headings seen at Internet subject trees. In terms of practical searching the symbolic pathway of notation has persistently failed. These failures have happened because searching via symbols has proved to be far too demanding for searchers' limited technical knowledge of classification schemes, and because it was too difficult for system operators to reveal the depth of meaning (relative index, cross references, scope notes, etc.) hidden behind their classification scheme's symbols.

Briefly, it's worth considering the implications of that last point in more detail. The alphabetical content (captions, scope notes, index entries, etc.) of a classification scheme is very considerable, but it's available only to classifiers, and not to searchers–whose needs are at least as great as classifiers' needs. In its day, the chain procedure index (which normally indexed classmarks, not the documents at the classmarks) tried to remedy this weakness. It alphabetically interpreted a classification scheme's content, especially its hierarchic content, and presented its interpretations to users. Whilst chain procedure indexes were far from perfect, they successfully insulated users from direct contact with the obscurities of symbolic notation and abstract hierarchy. Nevertheless, these indexes were often too rigidly defined or too loosely implemented, and were slow and difficult for users to search for serious information retrieval purposes, as was demonstrated in the Cranfield[1] and EPSILON tests.[21]

The benefits of the classificatory approach for Internet retrieval are most visibly realised in the Internet subject trees. With these, even large scale, complex and deep hierarchies having seven or more levels of headings, such as LookSmart and Yahoo, can be explored simply and successfully by users who have had no instruction, and who probably want no instruction. Unsurprisingly, the same is true of simpler and shallower hierarchies with just one or two levels, such as the ADAM[22] and OMNI[12] gateways. This simple and successful operation is possible because of three fundamental factors. Firstly, a widespread human grasp of hierarchy provides us with a jump-start for the task of browsing. Secondly, the browsing principle permits very simple searching without the necessity of posing a formal question. Thirdly, the progress of a browsing search at a subject tree is guided by an avalanche of feedback from the constant flow of site reviews on the screen.

The most reliable retrieval test relevant to subject trees is probably that of Borgman,[7] whose Science Library Catalog project reported similar performance levels for subject browsing and alphabetical index searching (she was working with children in controlled experimental conditions). However, this research was not directly an investigation of subject trees and its support must be viewed as being only tentative.

HOW DO END USERS USE CLASSIFICATION AND SUBJECT TREES?

If only we really understood the answers to this question! If anything, browsing a classification scheme or hierarchically organised headings at a subject tree is less understood than searching an alphabetical index. In truth, our knowledge of browsing activity amounts to scarcely more than loose observations and hearsay. We don't know what knowledge users typically have when they start using classified resources for searching. We know little about what makes users prefer browsing a classification scheme to searching an alphabetical index. We don't know what makes them start at one part of the classification scheme, or one subject heading, rather than another. We don't know why they accept one heading and reject related ones as they drill down through a hierarchy. We don't know what relative importance they attach to assigned subject headings, authors' titles, descriptive reviews, etc. We don't know what moves them to despair at one hierarchy and to pass hopefully on to another.

All that can be said with any confidence is that no survey of OPAC users has reported any significant use of the classified entries in the world's OPACs, but each day hundreds of thousands, perhaps millions, of users connect to the subject trees at Excite, Infoseek, LookSmart, Yahoo, etc. Furthermore, a very large percentage of these subject tree users will be sufficiently satisfied to return on later occasions. In particular, Yahoo (a search site where the subject tree has always been the principal search tool) holds a crushingly dominant position as the most visited Internet search site. StatMarket's figures repeatedly show Yahoo accounting for 40-50% of traffic from the major Internet search sites.[23] Can any OPAC or formally classified list of Internet resources claim this much impact on its users?

SO, WHAT ARE THE PROPERTIES OF TYPICAL INTERNET SUBJECT TREES?

Though individual subject trees, especially Yahoo, are frequently described in articles on Internet search engines, it is rare for a number of them to be described and compared, and the prime concern of authors[24-27] who do so has usually been the information content of subject trees and not their broad structure or classified organisation. The information in the two tables here, on the structure and postings of six popular subject trees, uses figures compiled by extrapolation from simple statistical counts. The samples were drawn in February 1999, and are in approximate agreement with other published figures or those extracted from site publicity material. Together they provide a summary picture of the better-known Internet subject trees. [I have preferred these figures for my comparisons because the vendors' figures do not seem to be calculated on any usefully equivalent basis.]

Apart from obvious differences in the scale of the subject trees, there is a surprising sameness in the figures. As Tables 1 and 2 show:

- The opening gambits of all subject trees are remarkably similar at about 12-20 top level headings.
- Except for Lycos Top 5%, the smallest subject tree examined, the general preference is to reserve top level headings for "announcing" the hierarchies below, and so there are almost no postings to

the top level headings. Presumably these headings are regarded as too general for most documents, but Lycos, which has fewer than one heading for every twenty found at the next largest subject tree, is forced to make greater use of its top level headings.

- Below this top level the patterns of headings and postings conform to roughly normal distributions.
- Except in Lycos Top 5%, two-thirds of the postings are concentrated levels 4 or 5, so searchers will usually have to browse down to these two levels before finding the documents they require.
- Specificity is similar in all the subject trees, with the notable exception of LookSmart whose specificity is only about one-third that of the others. It seems unlikely that the similarity is accidental, and the services must be exerting significant control to operate so consistently at this level. However, it is necessary to remember that the specificity figures shown in the Tables are averages, the reality is that individual headings can be found with one or hundreds of entries.
- LookSmart differs partly because of the lower average effective specificity of its headings, and partly because it posts documents only at the ends of its subject tree's "branches," a practice hidden by the presentation of Table 1 that merges the postings at shorter and longer branches. This posting practice helps users make best use of its interface but may ultimately present them with daunting arrays of entries. However, LookSmart's particularly graphical browsing interface (Figure 4) does much to hide its unusual postings distribution from users.
- Only the largest subject trees have adopted deep hierarchies, and the ones reported have apparently expanded their number of hierarchic levels only as their collection has expanded, so maintaining approximately similar specificity despite great variations of overall size. When extra levels are added, the amount of document space increases factorially, allowing large numbers of documents to be absorbed by very few extra hierarchic levels.
- Yahoo, though not the largest, is the only subject tree to make use of nine levels of heading. This secures the advantages of specificity for users, but at the price of an increased number of headings to be examined before a required document is likely to be found.

TABLE 1. Distribution of Headings in Six Internet Subject Trees

	Lycos Top 5%	Excite	Britannica e-BLAST	Infoseek GO Network	Yahoo	LookSmart
Number of postings	7,772	115,157	199,718	359,826	451,646	464,814
Number of headings	735	16,185	37,799	44,491	63,746	20,675
Specificity (postings per heading)	10.6	7.1	5.3	8.1	6.9	22.1
Level 1 headings	18	16	17	20	14	13
Level 2 headings	157	156	340	316	420	160
Level 3 headings	358	1,505	4,294	3,309	3,509	1,681
Level 4 headings	193	3,914	19,049	10,152	7,562	8,604
Level 5 headings	28	10,609	9,704	15,772	11,058	9,191
Level 6 headings	0	0	4,411	13,697	6,823	1,021
Level 7 headings	0	0	0	1,245	15,352	0
Level 8 headings	0	0	0	0	16,632	0
Level 9 headings	0	0	0	0	2,376	0

CONCLUSION

The convergence of so many publishers' minds on a common model of subject tree suggests either extreme plagiarism or a great confidence that this model of retrieval is what their customers want. Many of these publishers are mainstream commercial operators, not idiosyncratic members of the vanity press. If their customer research showed a subject tree to be unsuited to their customers needs, it would not stay as it is.

In this typical form, classificatory Internet subject trees are not rivals to the search engines, they complement the search engines–the former offer easy browsing of highly selective quality controlled databases, and the latter offer more formal searching of much larger databases distinguished by only the barest acquaintance with selectivity and quality control. Subject trees display their own unique properties, offering particular values for many information retrieval situations. Collecting together the most widely accepted views of their properties, it seems reasonable to claim that Internet subject trees:

- Provide "quality documents," pre-selected by human indexers

- Can be successfully searched without formal instruction
- Constantly provide the benefits of relevance feedback to aid search progress
- Require no knowledge of complex search commands
- Require no keyboard skills
- Require no formal search statement
- Provide copious in-search feedback
- Provide the advantages of browsing without the complexities of traditional bibliographic classification schemes
- Provide both alphabetical search vocabularies and hierarchic access without the formalities of the *Broader Terms* and *Narrower Terms* used by IR thesauri
- Are satisfactory for collections ranging from a few thousand to a few hundred thousand documents
- Can be developed to suit almost all ages of user
- Can be applied to multilingual collections

TABLE 2. Distribution of Postings in Six Internet Subject Trees

	Lycos Top 5%	Excite	Britannica e-BLAST	Infoseek GO Network	Yahoo	LookSmart
Number of postings	7,772	115,157	199,718	359,826	451,646	464,814
Number of headings	735	16,185	37,799	44,491	63,746	20,675
Specificity (postings per heading)	10.6	7.1	5.3	8.1	6.9	22.1
Postings at level 1	392	0	50	0	12	0
Postings at level 2	2,768	2,761	7,581	7,743	11,209	243
Postings at level 3	3,483	26,886	44,311	48,518	79,764	30,514
Postings at level 4	1,074	45,114	89,136	101,432	132,782	183,519
Postings at level 5	55	40,396	33,524	122,442	86,114	243,391
Postings at level 6	0	0	24,996	67,239	43,072	7,147
Postings at level 7	0	0	0	12,452	51,174	0
Postings at level 8	0	0	0	0	38,015	0
Postings at level 9	0	0	0	0	9,504	0

FIGURE 4. LookSmart made a significant and original advance in the presentation of subject hierarchies when they developed their "cascading" interface. But in the summer 1999 they appear to have had second thoughts, and their home site <http://www.looksmart.com> was converted to the conventional one-level-at-a-time approach, though the cascading interface remained in use at their UK localized site <http://www.looksmart.co.uk>. In use, the interface opens with just top level headings. It reveals second level headings only after a top level heading is chosen, reveals third level headings only after a second level heading is chosen, and so on (here, *Travel & Holidays > Scotland > General Guides*), and the user's path is highlighted by a white background. Since the interface always shows all alternative choices from each heading visited, it helps users to very easily review their search.

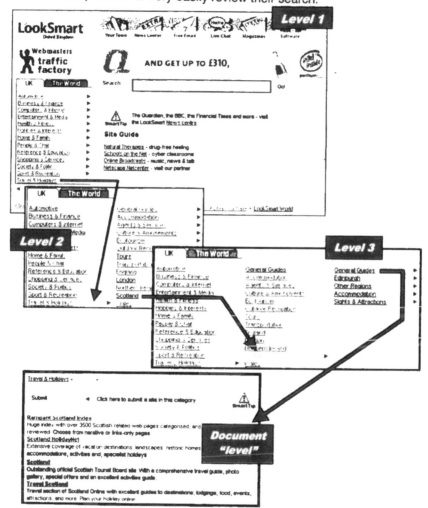

Lest this list should seem altogether too euphoric, two important points should be remembered.

- Subject trees have not been examined by performance testing such as that applied to many other information retrieval techniques.
- Today's Internet subject trees are created by human indexers, a far more expensive resource than the text search engines now dominating Internet information retrieval. It is also worth reflecting that the success of search engines probably owes much to the value of users' tolerance and relevance decisions as well as search engine retrieval powers.

NOTES

1. C.W. Cleverdon and J. Mills, "The testing of index language devices," *Aslib Proceedings* 15 (1963): 106-130.

2. C.W. Cleverdon, "The Cranfield test on index language devices," *Aslib Proceedings* 19 (1967): 173-194.

3. *Yahoo* [subject tree], URL: <http://www.yahoo.com/> (consulted 29th July 1999)

4. *Excite* [subject tree], URL: <http://www.excite.com/> (consulted 29th July 1999)

5. Karen M. Drabenstott and Marjorie S. Weller, "Failure analysis of subject searches in a test of a new design for subject access to online catalogs," *Journal of the American Society for Information Science* 47:7 (1996): 519-537.

6. Paula Busey and Tom Doerr, "Kids Catalog: An information retrieval system for children," *Journal of Youth Services in Libraries* 7:1 (1993): 77-84.

7. Christine L. Borgman, Sandra G. Hirsch, Virginia A. Walter, and Andrea L. Gallagher, "Children's searching behaviour on browsing and keyword online catalogs: The Science Library Catalog project," *Journal of the American Society for Information Science* 46:9 (1995): 663-684.

8. Traugott Koch, et al., *Specification for resource description methods. Part 3. The role of classification schemes in Internet resource description and discovery,* Desire Project Report 3.2, Lund: Lund University Library, 1997, URL: <http://www.ub2.lu.se/desire/radar/reports/D3.2.3/> (consulted 29th July 1999).

9. *Cyberstacks,* URL: <http://www.public.iastate.edu/~CYBERSTACKS/> (consulted 29th July 1999)

10. *LookSmart* [subject tree], URL: <http://looksmart.com/> (consulted 29th July 1999)

11. *EEVL*–Edinburgh Engineering Virtual Library [subject gateway], URL: <http://eevl.ac.uk/> (consulted 29th July 1999)

12. *OMNI*–Organising Medical Networked Information [subject gateway], URL: <http://omni.ac.uk/> (consulted 29th July 1999)

13. *PICK*–[subject gateway for Internet materials on library and information science], URL: <http://www.aber.ac.uk/~tplwww/e/> (consulted 29th July 1999)

14. K. Khan and C. Locatis, "Searching through cyberspace: The effects of link display and link density of information retrieval from hypertext on the World Wide Web," *Journal of the American Society for Information Science* 49:2 (1998): 176-182.

15. *Yep.com* [subject tree], URL: <http://yep.com> (consulted 29th July 1999)

16. N. Mitev, G. Venner, and S. Walker, *Designing an online public access catalogue*, Library and Information Research Report 39, London: British Library, 1985

17. *About the Open Directory Project*, <URL: <http://dmoz.org/about.html> (consulted 29th July 1999)

18. *Lycos and AOL's Netscape announce major Open Directory alliance*, URL: <http://www.lycos.com/press/opendirectory.html> (consulted 29th July 1999)

19. *Open Directory* [subject tree], <URL: <http://dmoz.org/> (consulted 29th July 1999)

20. Information displayed at Open Directory's home page, URL: <http://dmoz.o rg/> (consulted 29th July 1999)

21. E. Michael Keen and Alan Wheatley, *Evaluation of printed subject indexes by laboratory investigation*, Report to the British Library Research and Development Department 5454, Aberystwyth: College of Librarianship Wales, 1978.

22. *ADAM*–Art, Design, Architecture and Media Information Gateway [subject gateway], URL: <http://adam.ac.uk/> (consulted 29th July 1999)

23. StatMarket URL: *Top ten search engines.* <http://www.statmarket.com/> (consulted 29th July 1999)

24. Greg R. Notess, "Comparing net directories" *Database*, 20:1 (1997): 61-64.

25. Boyd R. Collins, "Webwatch" *Library Journal* 122:1 (1997): 31-32.

26. Alison Cooke, Alison McNab, and Betsy Agnostellis, "The good, the bad and the ugly: Internet review sites," *Online Information 96 Proceedings:* 33-40.

27. Thomas Pack, "Yahoo alternatives," *Database* 22:1 (1999): 51-54.

Classification Schemes Revisited: Applications to Web Indexing and Searching

Vanda Broughton
Heather Lane

SUMMARY. Basic skills of classification and subject indexing have been little taught in British library schools since automation was introduced into libraries. However, development of the Internet as a major medium of publication has stretched the capacity of search engines to cope with retrieval. Consequently, there has been interest in applying existing systems of knowledge organization to electronic resources. Unfortunately, the classification systems have been adopted without a full understanding of modern classification principles. Analytico-synthetic schemes have been used crudely, as in the case of the Universal Decimal Classification (UDC). The fully faceted Bliss Bibliographical Classification, 2nd edition (BC2) with its potential as a tool for electronic resource retrieval is virtually unknown outside academic libraries. *[Article copies available for a fee from The Haworth Document Delivery Service: 1-800-342-9678. E-mail address: getinfo@haworthpressinc.com <Website: http://www.haworthpressinc.com>]*

KEYWORDS. Classification, subject indexing, Internet resources, electronic resources, Bliss Bibliographic Classification, faceted classification

Vanda Broughton is a joint editor of the Bliss Bibliographic Classification, 2nd edition and is working on the revision of the Universal Decimal Classification (vanda.broughton@netscapeonline.co.uk).

Heather Lane, MA, ALA is Librarian, Sidney Sussex College, University of Cambridge, and Secretary of the Bliss Classification Association (hel20@cus.cam.ac.uk).

[Haworth co-indexing entry note]: "Classification Schemes Revisited: Applications to Web Indexing and Searching," Broughton, Vanda, and Heather Lane. Co-published simultaneously in *Journal of Internet Cataloging* (The Haworth Information Press, an imprint of The Haworth Press, Inc.) Vol. 2, No. 3/4, 2000, pp. 143-155; and: *Internet Searching and Indexing: The Subject Approach* (ed: Alan R. Thomas, and James R. Shearer) The Haworth Information Press, an imprint of The Haworth Press, Inc., 2000, pp. 143-155. Single or multiple copies of this article are available for a fee from The Haworth Document Delivery Service [1-800-342-9678, 9:00 a.m. - 5:00 p.m. (EST). E-mail address: getinfo@haworthpressinc.com].

143

During the 1980s and 1990s, interest waned among professional librarians and information workers in the traditional disciplines of classification and subject indexing. It was widely assumed that, in an electronic age, the speed of machine searching obviated the need for a systematic or structured approach to knowledge organization, since even the crudest software could process a search of the contents of enormous databases in a matter of seconds. In many library schools, conventional subject approaches to information management were substantially downgraded or abandoned in favour of IT skills acquisition. Professional expertise in the application of classification schemes and the construction of subject indexes and authorities was considered to be adequately conveyed in half a dozen sessions on the use of a major classification system.

At the same time on-line electronic resources continued to grow on a scale which could not have been imagined ten years before: there were estimated to be 3,689,227 WWW sites at the end of 1998.[1] By the mid-nineties there could hardly have been an academic library in the United Kingdom, from the largest university to the smallest rural primary school, which did not have an Internet connection, and the expectation that it would deliver usable teaching, learning, and research resources. And certainly it was easy to obtain results, for even with a minimum of search skills, hundreds and thousands of sites could be located. Nevertheless it soon became apparent that both the quality and the relevance of material retrieved was extremely variable, and that specificity in searching was hard to achieve.

It became clear that if the Internet and its resources were to be useful within the academic context, something akin to the conventional treatments adopted by librarians in the organization of print-based materials would need to be applied to the World Wide Web. As a consequence we began to see the development of directory style databases such as Yahoo,[2] which offered the user a systematic subject approach to information seeking, although the level of subject analysis was very rudimentary, and could hardly cope with complex subject enquiries in any satisfactory way.

An initial solution to the problem of quality control for the academic community was offered by the setting up of managed gateways in which the searcher would be offered links to sites of known value, each one investigated and assessed by librarians or subject specialists. A number of these gateways, ADAM,[3] SOSIG,[4] and EEVL,[5] were set up under the auspices of the British Library's eLib[6] programme and provide large structured databases of Websites of guaranteed usefulness. In the examples above, the electronic database can be seen to have parallels to the conventional library, in that the contents are selected for the user and made accessible to him through the medium of the conventional library classification scheme.

A number of schemes are currently being used in this way.[7] Sites using the Dewey Decimal Classification[8] include:

> Patrick's Subject Catalog
> <http://www.slac.stanford.edu/~clancey/dewey.html>
>
> The UK Web Library–searchable classified catalogue of UK Websites
> <http://scit.wlv.ac.uk/wwlib/newclass.html>
>
> CyberDewey: a guide to Internet resources organized using Dewey decimal classification codes
> <http://ivory.lm.com/~mundie/DDHC/DDH.html>

A site using Library of Congress Subject Headings[9] is

> CyberStacks
> <http://www.public.iastate.edu/~CYBERSTACKS/homepage.html>

The Universal Decimal Classification[10] is used by NISS.[11]

Subject specialist schemes such as that of the National Library of Medicine[12] have also been applied to managed gateways such as OMNI (Organizing Medical Networked Information) <http://www.omni.ac.uk>.

The conventional system of classification has very many obvious advantages for the Website organizer:

- it already exists so there is no need to re-invent the wheel. Those who have attempted the process of schedule construction and revision will appreciate the time required to develop systems even on a limited subject basis, and general systems of classification require decades of work because up-dating and restructuring form a continuous exercise

- up-dating facilities are in place and the systems are maintained by editorial staff
- these systems are familiar to the information professional, and in one form or another familiar to most users
- most are used on an international basis. The UDC in particular is available in a number of languages, and the notation can be used as a switching language, that is a standard for the exchange of terms and concepts across language divisions

Nevertheless, most can be criticised on a number of counts. Project DESIRE[13] has investigated several classification schemes, both general and special, which are widely used as resource organizers, and identified the operational shortcomings of each. The difficulties experienced by users of the system when inputting generally come under the following headings:

- the systems are not up-dated frequently enough for on-line use
- the hierarchical structure of the systems does not allow prominence for some recently developed areas, such as environmental studies
- the systems are too complex for easy use

In answer to this, it must be said that the 'traditional' schemes have been used in a 'traditional' style, that is for the purposes of 'marking and parking' primarily with the objective of allocating pre-co-ordinated classmarks, and normally at a fairly superficial level. Even in the case of systems such as UDC, which has a considerable analytico-synthetic capability, the tendency has been to utilise only the hierarchical superstructure of the system. Thus in the DESIRE documentation, it is stated the intention with one major information gateway[11] is not to go beyond the decimal point in its application of the UDC, thereby restricting its use to only 1000 possible classes, and ignoring entirely the potential of the system for flexible and sophisticated subject coding of documents. In the same study, the managers of OMNI criticised the requirement in UDC to synthesise classmarks for compound subjects. They wanted formal enumeration of all acceptable classmarks. This can only be viewed as a retrograde approach to classification and subject cataloguing, possibly indicating that the assignment of subject related metadata was carried out by untrained indexers.

The concept of 'knowledge' as a fixed and limited corpus, which can be analysed into successively smaller and smaller units in a fixed hierarchical or tree structure, dates back to the ancient world. Numerous examples of the structure of knowledge can be found, from the times of the Assyrians onwards; Aristotle in the classical period, mediaeval scholars such as Ramon Lull, and later Bacon, all produced systems based on the analysis of human knowledge. From a library science point of view, the original classification of Melvil Dewey[14] 'divides the field of knowledge into 9 main classes, numbered 1 to 9. Cyclopedias, periodicals, etc. . . . form a 10th class. Each class is similarly separated into nine divisions. . . . Divisions are similarly divided into 9 sections.'

Modern approaches to classification theory work from the premise that the subject description of a document should be synthesised from its constituent elements. Although useful for a scheme to utilise obvious semantic and taxonomic relationships, such as genus-species and synonymy, there is no rigid matrix or infrastructure of 'knowledge' into which 'topics' or 'subjects' can be inserted. Index entries need to be built from the ground up rather than directed down a hierarchy, and the complexity of links between both phenomena/entities and branches of knowledge/disciplines is such that tree structures are too limited a method to express adequately their diversity.

The fully faceted scheme of classification has been developed to allow this more modern approach to subject description, yet faceted schemes like BC2[15] have been largely disregarded as Web organizers. Yet BC2 offers its incomparably large vocabulary, capacity to operate both pre- and post-co-ordinately, and powerful functional capability as a search engine.

The faceted classification offers the following advantages over a traditional enumerative scheme:

- the vocabulary of a subject is analysed in terms of functional rather than taxonomic relationships
- therefore the individual components of the system exist in a context-free environment, until they are combined in a citation string
- there are no theoretical limits on the combinatorial capacity of the system, in terms of either the precision of the indexing (specificity) or the comprehensiveness (exhaustivity)
- given that the initial theoretical analysis of any area of information is accurately carried out, the system should be hospitable to any new 'subjects,' or any combinations of existing concepts or

those that might occur in the future, and should be capable of infinite expansion

- complex interrelationships between subjects can be accommodated, since the relationship of one term to another is not fixed at the outset by the schedule structure
- the system can be used pre- or post-co-ordinately, to generate either notational codes, or strings of subject descriptors
- there is an element of flexibility in the citation order of terms to allow for differing needs

BC2 is the only developed general system of classification built entirely on faceted principles. The first edition of the BC[16] was widely regarded as the most scholarly of all the schemes, with its philosophically based main class order, and capacity for systematic synthesis of compound classes through the medium of generally and specially applicable auxiliary schedules. In the 1960s a major programme of revision began, led by Jack Mills at the Polytechnic of North London Library School. Building on the infrastructure of the first edition, the revisers introduced an expanded and modernized terminology, analysed and organized according to facet-analytical principles, and incorporated many of the developments in classificatory theory which had resulted from the work of the Classification Research Group from the 1950s onwards. Published schedules for discrete main classes appeared from 1977 onwards, and the scheme is expected to be complete by 2003.

Despite the unparalleled soundness of its theoretical construction, the potential of BC2 as an organizer for Internet resources has been effectively unrecognized. It is an accessible universal classification which stands as a paradigm of a modern faceted classification scheme, and which has provided a theoretical model for the revision of other schemes, some more widely known. It provides a single comprehensive classification, which can be used at any level for metadata, either as selected subject descriptors or in the form of notation. It can also be used to organize any given search to maximise retrieval for a properly constructed search requires concept analysis whereby the information required is summarised into a set of terms or key words. The classification can then provide a tool for translation, arranging the terms of the summary into an order which reflects BC citation order. Ideally input of search terms can be made in natural language, matched if necessary against a controlled vocabulary.

All the elements which are required for these functions exist in BC2:

- there is a logical broad structure at the level of discipline and sub-discipline
- it provides a controlled vocabulary for subject description and searching
- the vocabulary is derived from natural language and has literary warrant
- the thesaurus facility links synonyms and near-synonyms
- each discipline is subject to fully faceted analysis
- the structure is non-hierarchical
- the provision of a retroactive synthetic notation with the ability to show compound classes is both elegant and economic

The main class order of BC2 is based on closely argued principles–that of gradation, supplemented by that of integrative level theory. The structure of each main class is organised by conceptual categories.

S. R. Ranganathan[19] first identified the categories PMEST (Personality, Matter, Energy, Space, Time). This categorization was subsequently developed (mainly by members of the UK Classification Research Group) into a standard citation or combination order. This citation order is generally employed in the construction of faceted schemes, and it recognises the 9 categories of 'thing'/entity–ind –part–property–process–operation–agent–space–time. It will be apparent that the standard citation order is one of decreasing concreteness. Within each main class of BC2, the vocabulary of a subject is analysed into these categories. Thus for Biology the result would be:

(Entity) e.g., Amphibians
- Kinds (e.g., frogs, newts, toads)
- Parts (e.g., heads, legs, lungs, digestive system)
- Properties (e.g., speed, longevity, colour)
- Processes [internal] (e.g., movement, respiration)
- Operations [by external agent] (e.g., dissection)
- Agents of action (e.g., zoologists)
- Space (e.g., Colombia)
- Time (e.g., 1999)

In constructing a *citation string* or *subject summary* for the theme of a particular document, the constituent parts are always written down in the above sequence. Consider the strings for (1) Reproduction in marine mammals, and (2) Design of carbon-fibre bicycle wheels in the UK. The analysis would be:

ENTITY	KIND	PART	PROPERTY	PROCESS	SPACE
1. Mammals	Marine			Reproduction	
2. Bicycles		Wheel	Carbon-fibre	Design	UK

The strings would be presented as:

1. Mammals–marine–reproduction
2. Bicycles–wheel–carbon-fibre–design–UK

(A further example is provided later after the abridged Biology schedule.)

The object of citation order is to produce a consistent arrangement and predictable location for any compound class. The indexer/classer (as well as an informed searcher) knows in which category the document will be placed. In our examples, (1) files with Mammals–not with marine or reproduction, (2) files with Bicycles–not with any of the other terms.

Although the term *category* is used to describe the general concepts of Property, Operation, Time, etc., within a particular subject context they are referred to as *facets*; so in Biology the *category* of Entity becomes the organisms or species *facet*, or in History the Time *category* becomes the period. The standard citation order discussed earlier is regarded as the optimum order for most subjects. However, there are some cases where it may usefully be varied (for example, in History, the first cited facet is Place).

When written down as a schedule, this order is *inverted*. That is, Time followed by Space, followed by Agent, etc., working downwards to specific entities at the end of the schedule, so that the more abstract concepts file first (on the shelves, or in a bibliography, card index, etc.). When building compound (multi-faceted) classes, every concept in the schedule may be qualified by any term preceding it, and the subject summary or citation string is composed *retroactively* by adding terms in the reverse of the schedule order, i.e., the term filing last is written first, and so on.

So, for our example of Biology, a highly abridged schedule would look like this:

Zoology
   (Time)
   (Space)
   (Agents)
      Persons. Zoologists
      Equipment. Microscopes
   (Processes)
      Growth
      Movement
      Reproduction
        Differentiation
      Pathology
      Disease
   (Properties)
   (Parts)
      Constituents
        Cells . . .
      Regional parts
      Head
      Limbs . . .
      Systems
        Nervous system
        Digestive system
   (Kinds/entities)
   Protozoa

   Fish
   Amphibians
      Toads
      Frogs . . .

So a document on 'Diseases of the nerve cells in frogs' would be summarised as:

Frogs–nervous system–cells–disease

and the compound class would file under Frogs, the qualifying classes being brought down under Frogs in the filing sequence (shelf or card-index order) as follows:

(Processes)
    Diseases of frogs (general)
(Parts)
    Cells
    Nervous system
        Nervous system cells
        (Processes)
            Diseases of nerve cells

It is true that the library classification scheme offers a purpose built solution to the problem of arranging the resources and sites of a gateway into a usable structure–but this only represents the top level of subject indexing.

It is important to understand that, in terms of practical classification the addition of notation to a subject description string is the final operation in the process of subject cataloguing, that notation is only necessary where a linear order is mandatory (e.g., on the library shelves or in a printed catalogue), and that it need be assigned only in such context. The end-user is very unlikely to search other than with subject 'keywords' of some sort–and will expect a keyword search to retrieve 'documents' whether from the library catalogue, the electronic database, or the World Wide Web.

Within the conventional library context the classification system will provide a source of subject descriptors through the medium of a controlled language database. The classification should form the basis of the subject authorities and indexes utilised in mechanised catalogues and databases, and so enabling efficient retrieval of documents to be performed. It is as a source of controlled vocabulary that the classification comes into its own. Its principal function is to generate subject descriptions for 'documents' (including Websites) using appropriate vocabulary in an ordered sequence. As such it can perform the 'marking and parking' function well, in that it can translate a complex subject expression to a structured string which will have a single predictable location.

In most cases, however, Internet searching will not be carried out on a database of pre-co-ordinated conceptual compounds, but rather one that offers full-text searching using keywords in conjunction with Boolean operators and proximity commands. A scheme like BC2 can be used in this situation to frame the search query, both by displaying the structure of the discipline (to provide context), and by offering a controlled vocabulary for the selection of appropriate keywords. In addition, the scheme can give guidance in the preferred subordination, or weighting, of terms, and indicate the range of possible compounds.

Used in this way, the notational encoding of the scheme is peripheral to the central exercise of subject analysis. Subject strings can theoretically be translated into any one of a variety of formal systems if a notational display is required, or they can be offered as alphabetical subject headings. They need not impose a structure of any sort on the database, being co-ordinated only at the time of search. An extensive, up-to-date, and rigorously analysed vocabulary can also be used as a central 'control' language from which subject strings can be mapped out onto the structure and notation of any other major system if desired.

A question needs to be asked about the realistic application of metadata. The use of classifications to date has required that subject linked metadata is assigned to sites by the gateway or database manager. Consequently only managed resources are accessible to the end-user via the medium of the classification, but managed sites are the minority. It is very unlikely that there will be widespread use of controlled schemes for incorporation in metadata fields. Commercial and organizational sites have no particular interest in doing this, it is a phenomenon predominantly related to academic use. Similarly, although metadata can be attached to sites by outside 'cataloguers,' the volume of work involved in covering even a tiny fraction of available sites means that this can only be a limited function of any system of resource subject management.

The relevance of a classification scheme to Website organization has to be in a multifunctional role–as in the conventional library context, where it operates as a tool for vocabulary control, for the generation of indexes, subject headings and authorities, for thesaurus construction, for the systematic arrangement of card and printed catalogues, for the provision of predictable locations in a linear sequence, and for use post-co-ordinately in the machine retrieval of indexed documents. Any or all of these functions are better performed by the fully faceted scheme as compared with hierarchical models of subject organization. Therefore it is to the faceted system of classification that we should look for a multi-role Web organizer–as a reservoir of subject oriented metadata, as a structuring tool for resource organization in managed gateways and databases, as a generator of subject strings for both storage and retrieval purposes, and as a yardstick for the mapping of subject based information across the barriers of languages.

Alongside this we need to re-discover and confirm those skills of intellectual analysis which have traditionally been the preserve of librarians and information specialists, and ensure that they are available to the current generation. Indexing and the subject approach to information was at one time the core of professional training. If we are to maintain a hold on the vast expanse of information available to us and to make that information accessible to the end-user at any and every level, we need to bring the subject approach back to centre stage. We need to promote those systems which represent the best in the field to the community at large.

REFERENCES

1. Alison Cooke, *A guide to finding quality information on the Internet* (London: Library Association Publishing, 1999) p.3.

2. Yahoo <http://www.yahoo.com> (1999) seen 30 Jul 1999

3. ADAM (Art, Design, Architecture and Media information gateway) <http://www.adam.ac.uk> (1999) seen 30 Jul 1999

4. *SOSIG (Social Sciences Information Gateway)* <http://www.sosig.ac.uk> (1999) seen 30 Jul 1999

5. *EEVL (Edinburgh Engineering Virtual Library)* <http://www.eevl.ac.uk> (1999) seen 30 Jul 1999

6. Electronic Libraries Programme, eLib <http://ukoln.ac.uk/services/elib/> seen 12 May 1999

7. Diane Vizine-Goetz, "Using library classification schemes for Internet resources", in Proceedings of the OCLC Internet Cataloguing Colloquium, San Antonio, Texas, 19 Jan 1996. <http://www.oclc.org/oclc/man/colloq/v-g.htm>

8. *Dewey decimal classification and relative index . . .* 21st ed. (Albany, N.Y.: Forest Press, 1996).

9. *Library of Congress Subject Headings*, 20th ed. (Washington D.C.: Library of Congress, 1997).

10. *Universal Decimal Classification*, English medium ed. (The Hague: UDC Consortium, 1994).

11. *NISS (National Information Services and Systems) Directory of Networked Resources* <http://www.niss.ac.uk> seen 30 Jul 1999

12. *National Library of Medicine Classification*, 4th ed. rev. (Bethesda, MD: U.S. Dept of Health and Human Services, 1981).

13. "The role of classification schemes in Internet resource description and discovery" *Work package 3 of Telematics for research project DESIRE (RE 1004)*

<http://www.ukoln.ac.uk/metadata/desire/classification/class_tc.htm> (14 May 1997) seen 12 May 1999

14. *Dewey Decimal Classification*, 3rd abridged ed. (New York: Forest Press, 1926). p.3.

15. Jack Mills and Vanda Broughton, eds., *Bliss Bibliographic Classification*, 2nd ed. (London: Bowker-Saur, 1977-).

16. H. E. Bliss, *A Bibliographic Classification* (New York: H. W. Wilson, 1940-1953). 4 vols.

SUBJECT CATALOGUING AND THE WORLD WIDE WEB

Attempt the end, and never stand to doubt:
Nothing's so hard, but search will find it out.

–Robert Herrick, *Hesperides: Seek and Finde,* 1648

Words without thoughts never to heaven go

–William Shakespeare, *Hamlet,* 1601?

Improving Subject Searching in Web-Based OPACs: Evaluation of the Problem and Guidelines for Design

Chris Evin Long

SUMMARY. Online catalog users search predominately by subject, yet it is the most difficult search to perform and retrieves records only about one-half of the time. A new generation of OPACs (online public access catalogs) is on the horizon, the Web-based OPAC. Web-based OPACs allow users to access online catalogs through a WWW (World Wide Web) interface and have the potential to improve patrons' ability to search by subject. But will this potential be realized? This article proposes some basic guidelines that can be incorporated into Web-based OPAC interface design to help users perform subject searches more effectively, and evaluates how well Web-based OPACs currently in operation address the subject searching problem. *[Article copies available for a fee from The Haworth Document Delivery Service: 1-800-342-9678. E-mail address: getinfo@haworthpressinc.com <Website: http://www.haworthpressinc.com>]*

KEYWORDS. World Wide Web, online catalogs, subject searching, online catalog design

Chris Evin Long is Catalog Librarian, School of Law, Indiana University–Indianapolis, 735 West New York Street, Indianapolis, IN 46202-5194 (clong@iupui.edu).

The author wishes to thank Wendell Johnting of the School of Law, Indiana University–Indianapolis, for his valuable suggestions in the preparation of this article.

[Haworth co-indexing entry note]: "Improving Subject Searching in Web-Based OPACs: Evaluation of the Problem and Guidelines for Design." Long, Chris Evin. Co-published simultaneously in *Journal of Internet Cataloging* (The Haworth Information Press, an imprint of The Haworth Press, Inc.) Vol. 2, No. 3/4, 2000, pp. 159-186; and: *Internet Searching and Indexing: The Subject Approach* (ed: Alan R. Thomas, and James R. Shearer) The Haworth Information Press, an imprint of The Haworth Press, Inc., 2000, pp. 159-186. Single or multiple copies of this article are available for a fee from The Haworth Document Delivery Service [1-800-342-9678, 9:00 a.m. - 5:00 p.m. (EST). E-mail address: getinfo@haworthpressinc.com].

159

INTRODUCTION

The threshold of a new millennium is an exciting place to stand. A time of both anticipation and reflection, it offers us a chance to look back on progress made thus far and to contemplate what has yet to be accomplished. This is especially true for the library community, to whom the advent of the WWW (World Wide Web) in recent years has presented numerous opportunities and challenges, although we are not always in agreement on how to pursue these new opportunities or which challenges to accept. A central theme to this debate, however, is the question: "How can we distill the essentials of our discipline, the knowledge of how information is produced, disseminated, and presented, and how people search for it and utilize it, and then apply this knowledge to the development of new information technology?"

Designers of OPACs (online public access catalogs) need to be pondering these issues as they stand on the threshold. Previous papers such as Large and Beheshti[1] and Beheshti[2] chronicle the history of OPAC development and research. Arising in the mid-1970s, the first-generation of OPACs offered very basic search capabilities using essentially the same bibliographic information and access points as the card catalog, often requiring character-by-character matching between what the user input and what the bibliographic record contained. Second-generation OPACs added such improvements as keyword searching, Boolean operators, and browsing functions.

But despite these improvements, studies (which will be referred to later) have consistently shown that OPAC users experience considerable trouble performing the most popular type of online catalog request, the subject search. Patrons are unable to translate their subject concepts into the subject vocabulary used in the catalog, retrieve either too many or too few records, and overall experience too many failed searches.

Threatening to compound this situation is the increasing breadth of information that OPACs contain. In the past, the contents of online catalogs were typically confined to a limited number of record types. Now, in addition to the library's bibliographic holdings and circulation records many OPACs include:

- community information and referral databases
- journal citation databases
- databases containing full-text journal articles

- reference databases
- images
- audio and visual files linked to bibliographic records
- remote access to other library catalogs, and
- connections to Internet resources.[3]

But despite the online catalog's expanding scope, Matthews has pointed out that "functionality of the OPAC remains essentially unchanged since the early 1980s."[4]

GUIDELINES FOR WEB-BASED OPACS

The Potential of Web-Based OPACs

Advances in computer technology and networking have led to the development of a new generation of online catalogs, Web-based OPACs. A Web-based OPAC is simply an online catalog that users access through a Web interface, and it offers a number of advantages over its text-bound predecessors. The hypertext model of information organization, browsing, and retrieval equips these Web-based catalogs to truly become a "one-stop shopping" center for the bibliographic records, full-text resources, and WWW links, thus enabling fuller exploitation of the information that OPACs already contain. A Web environment is especially conducive to accessing the digital data that is now being added alongside the traditional textual information. Searching in Web-based OPACs can be enhanced further through the application tools that are increasingly familiar to users like graphical devices (e.g., pull-down menus, windows, and icons) and search engines like those used on the Internet. Users are thus offered the prospect of creating searches that are more complex yet can be more flexibly and easily executed. Already deployed in a number of libraries, Web-based OPACs have the potential to alleviate some of the problems users encounter when searching by subject.

What is now needed are basic guidelines that can be incorporated into Web-based OPAC interface designs to help users perform subject searches–the predominant yet most troublesome online catalog request.

What Is Meant by Subject Searching?

In most OPACs topics can be searched using a controlled vocabulary or a keyword approach. *Controlled vocabulary* searching (also referred to in the literature as "exact term searching") pertains to the ability to use a controlled vocabulary (a thesaurus or list of subject headings) for subject access to the catalog. A *keyword* search (also known as "free-text searching" or "natural language searching"), on the other hand, looks for words that may appear in one or more fields of the record. Depending upon the system, the user may access documents which contain the specified word(s) anywhere in the record, he may be allowed to specify the fields in which the searching is to be performed, or he may be restricted to certain predefined fields.[5] Controlled vocabulary and keyword searches need not be thought of as being mutually exclusive. Many OPACs, for example, allow the user to perform a keyword search that is limited to controlled vocabulary fields. Yet another way that users can search for topics is by classification number.

In this article the phrase "subject searching" will be used in its broad sense, including controlled vocabulary, keyword, and classification number searching unless specifically noted otherwise.

Subject Searching Problems in the OPAC

The difficulty patrons encounter when executing subject searches in online catalogs is well-documented. Various studies have shown that users fail to retrieve any records in about half of all subject searches.[6] Reasons for this ineffectiveness include:

- users' inability to match their terminology with the subject system's terminology. Users are not familiar with the subject lists used in the catalog such as LCSH (Library of Congress Subject Headings)[7]
- users are unaware that they should use terms from a subject list when searching by subject[8]
- searches contain spelling and typographical errors[7]
- users do not understand or use Boolean logic[9]
- users do not know the subject area well[10]
- users do not know how to use the OPAC well.[10]

Keyword searching has often been touted as a cure-all for subject searching problems. OPAC developers incorporated these capabilities into their products as the limitations of offering controlled vocabulary searching alone became clear, and in fact Cherry[11] found that keyword searching does increase the likelihood that users will retrieve some records. Tillotson[12] revealed that if patrons had entered the same terms as keywords instead of subjects, they would have had more satisfactory results, although her study did not confirm that the users were happier when they used keyword searching.

However, two problems with keyword searching have been noted: they do not retrieve all the relevant items, and the number of irrelevant items retrieved greatly outnumber the relevant ones.[13] Furthermore Hildreth's study[14] showed that keyword searches, like subject heading searches, fail more often than not. Interestingly, the ability to execute searches of words contained within headings has been recognized as a powerful tool in aiding subject retrieval.[15]

That people have trouble searching by subject should not be surprising. As Borgman has made clear, users must employ three levels of knowledge when searching an OPAC:

- conceptual (translating an information need into a searchable query–e.g., "What terms should I use to find items on 'green marketing'?")
- semantic (how and when to use a system's features–e.g., "Should I use the *Find* or *Browse* command?")
- technical (basic computing skills and the syntax of entering queries as specific search statements–e.g., "Should I type *Smith John F.* or *John F. Smith*?").[15]

Or as Large and Beheshti put it, the "client must first conceptualize the need for information on a subject, then express that conceptualization in specific search terms, and match these terms against the terms used in the OPAC records to express subject aboutness." In addition, the user must have considerable knowledge of controlled vocabulary lists like LCSH to be consistently successful.[1] Couple this with Borgman's observation[15] that most users are perpetual novices at searching OPACs, and it is easy to see why subject searching is such an unproductive task for most library patrons.

Design Guidelines to Improve Subject Searching

A significant body of research into online catalog searching behavior exists but, as Borgman laments, very little of it has informed the design models of the online catalogs developed thus far.[15] In the face of robust OPACs enriched with a multitude of variegated information sources, we ignore this knowledge at our peril. Despite the presumptuousness and futility of trying to take aim at such a fast-moving target as Web-based OPAC development, a list of guidelines now follows that should be incorporated into the design of Web-based catalogs. This list may be useful as a starting point in improving patrons' ability to perform the subject search, which remains the most common yet most difficult OPAC problem.

Accessibility

1. A text-based interface should be available.
2. Avoid over-reliance on graphical devices for searching functions.
3. The Web interface should be designed with some consideration for the disabled.

Search Environment

4. Both keyword and subject heading search options should be available and prominently displayed on the initial search page.
5. Labels for the search options should clearly convey the type of search that will be performed.
6. The user should be told what fields in the bibliographic record will be searched in the keyword option.
7. Users doing a subject heading search should be told that their search terms must match the terms used in a subject list.
8. Users should be told what subject list(s) is used in the catalog.
9. The subject list used in the catalog should be searchable online.
10. Users should be given alternative ways to search by subject, such as keyword searches restricted to subject fields and the ability to search by classification number.
11. The catalog should include search features that incorporate the entire cross-reference structure of subject headings.
12. Retrieved records should contain subject heading hyperlinks to other records with the same subject headings.
13. The user's search terms should be highlighted in retrieved records.

Help Features

14. Context-sensitive online instructions on how to perform keyword and subject heading searches should be available.
15. Help instructions for keyword and subject heading searching should incorporate conceptual aspects of searching in addition to procedures.
16. Assistance should be offered if no records are retrieved.
17. Assistance should be offered even if some records are retrieved.

Discussion of Guidelines

Accessibility

The ability to add graphical elements to the OPAC is definitely one of the most attractive features of Web-based OPACs. It is readily familiar to even casual users of Windows, Apple Macintosh, and the Internet. This is a prime consideration since we know that OPAC searchers expect systems to be easy to use with relatively little time invested.[15] But one can have too much of a good thing–as Dowling points out, Web interface creators often design interfaces that are clumsy or even useless in text-only browsers. This will automatically exclude a certain percentage of patrons who, through preference or necessity, use the text-only Lynx browser (*Guideline 1*). If icons are used as searching devices, then either their meaning should be readily discernible or explanatory text should be imbedded in or located in close proximity to them so as to avoid confusing the patron (*Guideline 2*).

Neglecting text-based alternatives will also result in the exclusion of the visually impaired, since screen-reading software that can interpret graphical environments is still experimental and not likely to be widely available for some time.[16] Another consideration is screen layout relative to screen size. Interface designers would do well to minimize the amount of scrolling needed to view the contents of a "page." Having a layout larger than the screen size means that the user is not aware of all that is on the page. This is particularly a problem when searching instructions or "help" features are buried at the bottom of the page, out of sight at the point where the user conducts the search. This has also been shown to be an obstacle for motor-impaired clients, who work more easily with interfaces that require the least amount of scrolling (*Guideline 3*).[17]

Search Environment

Tillotson showed that, given an easy choice, people will choose to use both keyword and controlled vocabulary searching,[8] so both should be available on the first page of search options. Studies have also shown that factors such as menu sequence (the order in which search options are offered) will affect user selection.[1] Users are more apt to choose an option higher rather than lower in the list, so it makes sense to prominently display the two options that will probably be most effective (*Guideline 4*).

Most OPAC users have little understanding of how the system processes their requests.[18] Hsieh-Yee[19] and Connaway, Johnson, and Searing[20] have found evidence that users are also confused about the difference between a keyword and a subject heading search. The labels used to identify various search options should be specific enough for users to make an appropriate choice (*Guideline 5*). Furthermore, patrons should be told what parts of the bibliographic record will be searched for keywords to give them some idea of the scope and limitations of their search (*Guideline 6*).

One-half of the users in Tillotson's study were unaware they should use LCSH when conducting a subject search. This outcome should not be surprising because less than one-half of the OPAC interfaces that she evaluated explained what was going on when an exact term search was performed. No mention was made of the fact that a subject list was being searched and that using the terms from that list might produce better results.[8] Users should be told not only that their subject heading search terms are drawn from a controlled vocabulary list, but also what list is being used, that this list can be searched separately, and where the list can be found (*Guidelines 7-8*).

Focus group interviews by Connaway, Johnson, and Searing[21] revealed that students liked having the ability to search an online thesaurus of subject terms to modify or narrow their searches, so ideally a hyperlink to the library's subject list should be incorporated into Web-based OPACs as well (*Guideline 9*).

The interviews also showed that users greatly desire approaches to searching by subject that go beyond the basic subject heading search, specifically mentioning call number searches.[21] As mentioned earlier, the ability to search subject heading fields by keyword has also been shown to increase the likelihood of successful subject retrieval (*Guideline 10*).

The focus group participants also recommended that OPACs be enhanced by adding subject cross-references and by automatically matching incorrect headings to LCSH terms. Furthermore, Connaway, Johnson, and Searing[21] and Hsieh-Yee[19] both report that searchers examine the subject headings in records they have already retrieved to further modify or refine their subject requests. Providing hypertext links, then, to preferred terms (i.e., terms included in the controlled vocabulary) when non-preferred terms are entered, to broader, narrower, and related terms, and to other records containing relevant subject headings is one of the most useful features that Web-based OPAC interface designers can add (*Guidelines 11-12*). Highlighting the search terms entered by patrons using color and/or different font styles may also help them determine the relevance of the retrieved item (*Guideline 13*).

Help Features

Hildreth found that users in his study preferred to seek assistance first from library staff, secondly from a nearby catalog user, thirdly from online "help" screens, and lastly from printed instructions.[22] With the number of remote users growing and likely to increase even more, though, the opportunity to ask a librarian or a nearby fellow searcher will diminish greatly, and most of the instructions will have to be online. Interestingly, though, almost all of these same users said they would like the catalog to indicate when a keyword search is preferable. Hildreth concludes that users "seem to prefer contextual, point-of-need, search stage-sensitive assistance." Searching instructions, therefore, should be online, available in some fashion at the point-of-search (whether it be the instructions themselves or a clickable link to them), and ideally geared to the type of search the user wants to do (*Guideline 14*).

Borgman asserts that OPAC users need more help with the conceptual aspects of subject searching than with the procedural.[15] Tillotson notes that unfortunately most online catalogs do very little in the way of explaining the use of controlled vocabulary.[8] Searching instructions should therefore include guidance to users on how they can translate their ideas into terms used in the catalog, together with guidance on technical skills such as how to enter a search request (*Guideline 15*).

Tillotson[8] contends that most online catalogs offer little or no help with unsuccessful searches. This is a design flaw that should not transfer to Web-based OPACs. Hildreth[23] goes so far as to say that the first principle of OPAC design should be that a user's search attempt should never fail to retrieve one or more bibliographic records for review; *something* should always be retrieved for display and review. In general, a search attempt may fail to retrieve any records for the following reasons:

- there are no relevant items in the database
- the search technique was poor
- the search was too narrow.

If the database contains no relevant records, then the correct response was achieved and offering help is inappropriate. If no records are returned because of poor search technique, then general help in constructing searches is needed. If the search was too narrow, however, the user needs guidance on how to broaden the search.

The designer is therefore faced with a dilemma–how is the system to determine which of the three possibilities is the correct one and give the appropriate response? Until OPACs reach this level of sophistication, it may be best to take a utilitarian approach. At minimum, searchers who have retrieved no records should be given basic hints on how to construct or broaden a search (*Guideline 16*). Ideally, this information would incorporate conceptual aspects of subject searching (*Guideline 15*). While offers of assistance may be irritating to the experienced searcher whose request has properly returned no records, this inconvenience is offset by the amount of good that such guidance can do for less skillful users.

Some form of help should also be offered even if the searcher does retrieve some records, because these records may not satisfy the patron's information needs (*Guideline 17*).

EVALUATION OF SUBJECT SEARCHING
IN WEB-BASED OPACS

Methodology

The author therefore conducted a critical evaluation of the subject searching capabilities of sixty Web-based OPACs. A checklist (Appendix 1) was constructed around the issues discussed in the preceding seventeen guidelines and informed by the known online subject searching problems discussed earlier. The checklist consisted of three parts:

- general OPAC design (availability of text-based interfaces; availability of both keyword and subject search options; search icons)
- keyword searching (labels; fields searched; presence, proximity, and quality of instructions; hyperlinks; help)
- subject heading searching (labels; user's awareness of subject lists; presence, proximity, and quality of instructions; keyword searching of subject headings; application of subject heading cross-reference structure; help).

Most of the questions were designed to be answered yes or no, with a few of necessity being left open-ended to account for unforeseeable variations among different sites. Some modifications were made to the checklist as the evaluation progressed, most occurring after a pilot test involving four Web-based OPACs and a few occurring in the early stages of the real evaluation.

Sixty sites having functional Web-based OPACs were chosen (Appendix 2). They were selected from Peter Scott's *webCATS: Library Catalogues on the World Wide Web* (http://www.lights.com/webcats/). In selecting the sites, an attempt was made to include Web-based OPACs from as many different vendors as possible and to include a mixture of academic, public, and special library sites. Every vendor that had at least one site in the United States was included. In addition, 9 sites listed under Scott's home-grown or unknown category were selected. The breakdown of vendors is as follows:

- 5 vendors having 50+ U.S. sites: 6 each (3 academic, 2 public, 1 special if possible) for a total of 30
- 1 vendor having 25-49 U.S. sites: 4 (2 academic, 1 public, 1 special if possible)
- 8 vendors having 1-24 U.S. sites: 1-2 each depending on availability for a total of 13
- 4 vendors representing consortia that shared the same interface: 1 each for a total of 4;
- 9 interfaces identified as home-grown or unknown.

The evaluations were performed from June 23 to July 2, 1998 using Netscape Communicator 4.0. It should be borne in mind that the purpose of these evaluations was to see how well the design of these Web-based OPACs addressed the problem of subject searching; they were not meant to be a vendor-to-vendor comparison of different products or a library-to-library comparison of how the catalogs were implemented.

See Tables 1 and 2 for responses to the questionnaire.

Discussion of Survey Results

Accessibility

The survey results suggest that most libraries are doing a good job of providing access to search options and instructions that is quick and comprehensible. All of the libraries that employed icons having search functionality included explanatory text within or in close proximity to the icon, so users did not have to guess as to what their purpose was (*Question 1.3.2*). Furthermore, a large majority of libraries that provided instructions on how to perform keyword and subject heading searches placed either the instructions themselves or a clickable link to them within the user's eyesight as he was performing a search (*Questions 2.3.1, 3.4.1*). The remaining libraries forced the user to either scroll down the page or consult a general "help" page for the directions.

On a less positive note, more libraries should consider providing a text-based alternate to the Web-based OPAC (*Question 1.1*).

Search Environment

A large majority of libraries included both keyword and subject heading search options on the initial search page (*Question 1.2*). This is not surprising because these methods have been OPAC staples for years. Only 1 site defaulted to a keyword search and gave the user no other options.

Two questions included in the checklist but not listed in the table involved search option labeling. Since catalog users are often confused about the difference between keyword and subject heading searching, it was deemed advisable that search option labels clearly convey the type of search to be performed. A few provided no labels.

TABLE 1. Showing the Total Responses of the Various Sites to the Questionnaire Questions

Q No.	Question	Guideline Numbers	Totals	%
1.1	Is a text-based interface also offered?	1,3	19/60	32
1.2	Are both keyword and subject heading search methods offered on the initial search page?	4	52/60	87
1.2.1	If not, is only keyword searching offered on the initial search page?		4/60	7
1.2.2	If not, is only subject heading searching offered on the initial search page?		4/60	7
1.3	Are search icons used?	2	22/60	37
1.3.1	Is the icon's meaning readily discernible independent of any accompanying text?		10/22	45
1.3.2	Is explanatory text contained within and/or in close proximity to the icon?		22/22	100
2.2	Is there an indication of what fields in the bibliographic record may be searched in a keyword search?	6	33/59*	56
2.3	Are there instructions on how to perform a keyword search?	14	51/59	87
2.3.1	Are these instructions in close proximity to the point-of-search?	3	43/51	84
2.3.2	Do instructions/HELP features incorporate conceptual aspects of searching in addition to procedures?	15	10/51	20
2.4	Are search words highlighted in retrieved bibliographic records?	13	12/59	20
2.5	Are hypertext links provided for subject headings in the bibliographic record?	12	51/59	86
2.6	For searches that retrieve at least 1 item, is help offered if the user is unsatisfied?	17	1/59	2
2.7	For searches that retrieve zero hits, are there suggestions for improving the search?	16	12/59	20
	OPAC prompts for keyword searches that retrieve zero hits:			
	User might try a subject search		0/12	0
	User might try the same search with suggested variations		3/12	25
	User might check for technical errors (spelling, using proper buttons, letter case, etc.)		11/12	92
	User provided with or directed to search hints		9/12	75
	User might ask a librarian		3/12	25
	No suggestions–user taken to a list of terms in the alphabetical neighborhood of the query		14/47	30
	No suggestions–user may enter a new search or select another search option		20/47	43
3.2	Are users told that subject search terms must match terms from a subject list?	7	21/60	35
3.3	Are users told which subject list(s) is used in the catalog?	8	20/60	33
3.3.1	Is the subject list searchable online?	9	2/60	3

TABLE 1 (continued)

Q No.	Question	Guideline Numbers	Totals	%
3.4	Are there instructions on how to perform a subject heading search?	14	43/60	72
3.4.1	Are these instructions in close proximity to the point-of-search?	3	38/60	63
3.4.2	Do instructions/HELP features incorporate conceptual aspects of subject heading searching in addition to procedures?	15	2/60	3
3.5	Is keyword searching of subject headings offered?	10	27/60	45
3.5.1	For keyword searches limited to subject headings that retrieve at least 1 item, is help offered if the user is unsatisfied?	17	0/28	0
3.6	Is classification number searching offered?	10	35/60	58
3.7	Are there search features that incorporate the subject heading's cross-reference structure?	11	30/60	50
3.7.1	Are "see" references hyperlinked to bibliographic records containing the correct subject heading?	11	29/30	97
3.7.2	Are there hyperlinks to bibliographic records containing broader, narrower, or related terms?	11	27/31	87
3.8	For searches that retrieve zero hits, are there suggestions for improving the search?		9/60	15
	OPAC prompts for subject heading searches that retrieve zero hits:			
	User might consult a subject list		2/10	20
	User might try a keyword search		3/10	30
	User provided with or directed to search hints		3/10	30
	User might check for technical errors (spelling, using proper buttons, letter case, etc.)		9/10	90
	User might ask a librarian		4/10	10
	No suggestions–user is taken to a list of subject headings in the alphabetical neighborhood of the query		25/50	50
	No suggestions–user may enter a new search or select another search option		14/50	28

*1 site did not offer keyword searching

For keyword searching (*Question 2.1*), most libraries used names one might expect like the generic "Keyword(s)," "Keyword Search," and "Word/Phrase," or the more specific "Title/Author/Subject Keyword." Some sites, though, chose labels like "Express," "All Indexes," and "All Headings." While librarians and other experienced OPAC searchers might understand these terms, they may be too vague for more casual users.

Ideally, labels for subject heading search options should give some intimation that the client must use precise terms from a controlled

TABLE 2. Showing the Grouped Responses by Specific Vendors to Each Questionnaire Question

VENDOR	NO OF SITES	QUESTIONNAIRE QUESTION NUMBER																											
		1.1	1.2	1.2.1	1.2.2	1.3	1.3.1	1.3.2	2.2	2.3	2.3.1	2.3.2	2.4	2.5	2.8	2.7	3.2	3.3	3.3.1	3.4	3.4.1	3.4.2	3.5	3.5.1	3.6	3.7	3.7.1	3.7.2	3.8
Ameritech	6	4	6						6	2	1	1		5		2	1	1		1	1	1	4						2
DRA	6	3	6			1	1	1	4	5	4	2		6	1		3	3		4	4	1	1	1	5	4	4	4	
Endeavor	6	2	3		3	6	6	6	1	6	6		6	6		1	2	2		6	6				6	6	5	6	2
Innovative Interfaces	6	3	6			1		1	6	6	6	2	4	5			4	3		6	6				6	5	5	5	
SIRSI	6	1	6			3	1	3	1	6	6			6			2	2		4	4				6	3	3	3	
VTLS	4	4	4			4		4		4	4			4		4				4	4		4		4	2	2	1	
Brodart	2	1	1						2	2	2			2									2		1	2	2		
Gaylord	2	2	2			2	2	2	2	2	2									2	2				2	2	2		
Geac	2		2			2		2	2	2				2						2			2		2	1			
Inmagic	2	1	1						1	2	2									1	1		1						
Nichols Advanced Technology	2	2							2	2	2	2	2	2						2	2								
Unknown/home-grown/others	16	6	15	1		3		3	8	12	8	3		13		4	9	9	2	11	8	1	13		5	5	5	4	5

(NB: Full data for each site surveyed may be obtained from the author or the editors)

vocabulary list (*Question 3.1*). Most of the sites used general words and phrases like "Subject," "Subject Searching," and "Subject Heading." One library even labeled their subject heading option with the vague "Terms." Several libraries, though, used more detailed phrases like "Subject Heading, Exact," "Subject LC/MeSH," and "Exact Subject." Specific labels such as these are more likely to convey the notion that appropriate subject heading search terms must come from a subject list.

The evaluation also showed that many libraries can do a better job of explaining to users how their keyword and subject heading searches will be processed. Although 56% of the sites gave the patron some indication as to which fields would be searched if a keyword search was executed, this information was sometimes buried in a help screen (*Question 2.2*). A much smaller percentage saw fit to explain to their users that they must use terms from a subject list when performing a subject heading search (*Question 3.2*). An even smaller number identified the list(s) used by the library (*Question 3.3*). Only 2 libraries mounted an online searchable version of LCSH and Library of Congress authorities, and use was restricted to patrons from subscribing institutions (*Question 3.3.1*).

A number of other approaches to subject heading searching were present in the Web-based OPACs that were evaluated. Allowing searchers to locate items on a relevant subject with the ease of clicking on a hypertext link is one of the most useful characteristics of a Web-based OPAC (*Question 2.5*). This fact has apparently not been overlooked by interface designers, since 86% of the sites included this feature. For some DRA (Data Research Associates) libraries, though, this feature was only available if the records were displayed in their full form. The Nichols Advanced Technology interface contained a curious hyperlink component: users are able to click on individual parts of a subject heading rather than having the hyperlink include the whole subject heading. This might be helpful in searching a very narrow subdivision like " . . .–Civil War, 1861-1865" but less useful for a very general subdivision like " . . .–History."

Several systems permitted the user to browse subject headings. Browsing a list of subject headings is undoubtedly simpler for most patrons than trying to determine the preferred term, but may prove ineffective if the subject system's cross-reference structure is not incorporated into the display. Users who enter terms that are alphabetically close to the preferred heading may be placed close enough to find it. On the other hand, if the client's term is nowhere near the preferred heading, browsability is of little value without reference to the preferred term.

Almost half of the Web-based OPACs offered subject heading keyword searching, although one library's catalog made no mention of it–it was discovered by serendipity (*Question 3.5*). As with broader keyword searches, there is the danger of retrieving too many irrelevant items. A number of systems sought to correct this by permitting the set of retrieved records to be limited, modified, or refined. A larger number of sites offered the option of searching by classification number (*Question 3.6*).

Users want to be directed to the correct form of subject headings and to related topics, and the Web catalogs of half the libraries accommodated them in varying degrees (*Question 3.7*). All but one provided hyperlinks to preferred terms when non-preferred terms were entered, although a close evaluation revealed that several catalogs only did this for some headings (*Question 3.7.1.*). OCLC's system was the only one that bypassed the hyperlink method and transparently took the user to records containing the correct form of heading.

Twenty-seven of the 31 libraries also linked users to broader, narrower, or related terms present in the subject heading's reference structure (*Question 3.7.2*). The breakdown is as follows:

- 5 provided links to all terms
- 9 provided links to narrower and related terms only
- 7 provided links to broader and related terms only
- 4 provided links to narrower terms only
- 1 provided links to broader terms only
- 1 provided links to related terms only.

A couple of innovations discovered in several of the SIRSI catalogs are noteworthy. One is a very useful "X-ref" icon that allows users to search all cross-references. A second is the linkage even in keyword searches of "see" references to the proper LCSH.

A few flaws in some of the systems were also detected. As was the case with "see" references, the hyperlinks in several systems worked for some headings and not others. Also, in two systems the cross-reference links were only activated if an invalid term was used; the hyperlinks were not activated if a correct LCSH was entered, thereby depriving users of the additional broader, narrower, or related terms.

Help

It should go without saying that OPACs ought to contain instructions on how to perform keyword and subject heading searches. It was disappointing that even a small number like 13% of the libraries offering keyword searching failed to provide any instructions (*Question 2.3*). Advice on how to search by subject heading is even more important, so it was disheartening to see that an even greater percentage (28%) failed to offer any guidance on how to perform a subject heading search (*Question 3.4*). On a more positive note, the vast majority of libraries that did provide instructions recognized the value of placing them in close proximity to the point of search (*Questions 2.3.1 & 3.4.1*).

Instructions and "help" features are areas in which some of the misunderstandings between keyword and subject heading searching can be dispelled. Admittedly, *Questions 2.3.2 and 3.4.2* are very subjective questions. In general, it seemed that instructions which warranted a "yes" answer to *Question 2.3.2* should go beyond merely explaining the basic mechanics of how to do a keyword search. Instead, *conceptual* directions for keyword searches should include topics like detailed explanations of the fields to be searched, limiting by certain criteria, Boolean operators, truncation, wildcards, and searches that combine multiple fields. To varying degrees, 75% of libraries offering keyword instructions provided directions that incorporated conceptual aspects of searching.

Similarly, it seemed that sets of instructions deserving an affirmative answer to *Question 3.4.2* should include a description of the subject list(s) used by the library, a detailed explanation of how to use the subject list(s), guidance on how to translate these subject terms into an online request, and advice on what to do if no items were retrieved. Only two libraries met this criteria. When contrasted with the number of sites providing conceptually-based keyword instruction, it is apparent that libraries are inconsistent as to the quality of help offered the keyword searcher and the subject heading searcher.

The survey results corroborate Tillotson's contention that most online catalogs offer little or no assistance with either unsuccessful keyword or subject heading requests. Only a few provided any sort of help when keyword searches retrieved nothing (*Question 2.7*). The most common prompt (present in 11 sites) was for the user to check for technical errors, such as spelling or use of the proper search button. Nine sites provided users with or directed them to search hints. Three libraries suggested that the user try the same search with suggested variations, and 3 suggested that the user ask a librarian. None of the sites suggested that the user consider a subject heading search. Forty-seven (80%) sites offered no suggestions. Fourteen took the patron to a list of terms in the alphabetical neighborhood of the query, and 20 allowed the user to enter a new search or to select another search option. The Web-based OPACs in 15 libraries gave no prompts at all.

Likewise, only a small minority (15%) of sites offered suggestions on how the patron might improve a subject heading search that retrieved no hits (*Question 3.8*). The most common prompt (present in 9 sites) was for the user to check for technical mistakes, such as mis-spellings and using incorrect search buttons. Four catalogs suggested that the user ask a librarian–a useful strategy although no help for a remote user. Three catalogs provided the user with search hints. Two of the most likely strategies to produce results went largely unmentioned: only 3 systems suggested that the patron try a keyword search and only 2 suggested consulting a subject list! No libraries suggested trying a keyword subject heading search even though many of their catalogs offered that capability. Fourteen of the 50 catalogs that offered no suggestions merely provided the user with an opportunity to enter a new search or select another option. More significantly, 25 of these 50 catalogs took the user to a list of subject headings in the alphabetical neighborhood of the query. Some people may consider this helpful though it is of limited value if the preferred term is not related to any of the subject headings in the list returned.

It is presumptuous to suppose that a search is successful simply because it retrieved at least one record, for the user may feel that none of the items are relevant. This has seldom been a feature offered in online catalogs so it is not surprising that not one library provided this in the Web-based OPACs (*Questions 2.6 & 3.5.1*). However, several systems (DRA, Geac, Innovative Interfaces, PALS [Georgia], Web-PALs [Minnesota] and WebPALS [South Dakota]) did allow users to refine or limit their search if they were dissatisfied with the results. Endeavor included a relevance ranking component. OPAC designers should reconsider this issue and provide some connection to help in the event that a user is dissatisfied with their search results.

CONCLUSION

Researchers have brought to light a great deal of information regarding the searching habits of online catalog users, especially the difficulties encountered when performing a subject search. The next generation of online catalogs, the Web-based OPACs, has the potential to improve the patron's lot in this area. Internet-savvy clients can access an online catalog teeming with diverse information resources through a Webbed interface that employs familiar devices like icons, hypertext links, and search engines. The Web environment makes possible a number of subject searching enhancements, including:

- the availability of point-of-search, context-specific instructions
- the introduction of relevance-ranking components and other features that improve retrieval quality by allowing users to more easily limit and modify their searches
- the use of hypertext links to guide patrons to other records with the same subject headings, to the correct form of subject headings, and to broader, narrower, and related terms
- the ability to browse a list of subject terms online
- and even the capability to search an online list of subject headings.

An evaluation of Web-based OPACs currently in operation, though, shows that many deficiencies present in earlier generations of online catalogs have been passed down to the next generation. The Web-based catalogs that were examined did little to clear up the confusion between keyword and controlled vocabulary searching; less than 40% explained what subject list was used or that subject heading search terms must come from that list. Nor did many libraries provide online access to their subject list(s). A few allowed the user to browse subject headings alphabetically, but only two offered the much more helpful option of online searching of the subject heading list itself.

The assistance offered to users by Web-based catalog designers in formulating sound search strategies and guiding patrons to success when their searches fail is another area that must be improved. Few systems provide users with directions on how they can translate their subject concepts into subject heading terminology; some offer no instructions at all. While most sites use hypertext links to improve subject searching, only a very small number take full advantage of the subject headings' cross-reference structure. When the client's subject search fails, as it probably will half the time, only a small minority of libraries offer suggestions on how the search might be improved.

Furthermore, the majority of libraries are in danger of excluding the technologically-deprived by failing to provide a text-based alternative to their Web-based OPAC, and of hampering the ability of visually- and motor-impaired patrons to use their catalog by constructing inter- face designs that do not take into account the needs of these groups.

As we stand on the threshold of a new era of online catalog devel- opment, all of us who have some influence on the design of Web- based OPACs should use the various opportunities available to im- prove the ability of our patrons to perform their subject searches.

NOTES

1. Andrew Large and Jamshid Beheshti, "OPACs: A Research Review," *Library & Information Science Research* 19:2 (1997): 111-113.

2. Jamshid Beheshti, "The Evolving OPAC," *Cataloging & Classification Quarterly* 24:1-2 (1997): 163-185.

3. Joseph R. Matthews, "Time for New OPAC Initiatives: An Overview of Landmarks in the Literature and Introduction to WordFocus," *Library Hi Tech* 15:1-2 (1997): 111-122.

4. as 3. p.111.

5. Maja Zumer and Lei Zung, "Comparison and Evaluation of OPAC End-User Interfaces," *Cataloging & Classification Quarterly* 19:2 (1994): 67-98.

6. as 3. p. 112.

7. Martha M. Yee, "System Design and Cataloging Meet the User: User Inter- face to Online Public Catalogs," *Journal of the American Society for Information Science* 42:2 (1991): 78-98.

8. Joy Tillotson, "Is Keyword Searching the Answer?" *College & Research Li- braries* 56:3 (1995): 199-206.

9. as 7. p.94.

10. as 1. p.112.

11. Joan M. Cherry, "Improving Subject Access in OPACs: An Exploratory Study of Conversion of Users' Queries," *Journal of Academic Librarianship* 18:2 (1992): 95-99.

12. as 8. p. 206.

13. Jennifer Rowley, "The Controlled Versus Natural Indexing Languages Debates Revisited: A Perspective on Information Retrieval Practice and Research," *Journal of Information Science* 20:2 (1994): 108-119.

14. Charles R. Hildreth, "The Use and Understanding of Keyword Searching in a University Online Catalog," *Information Technology and Libraries* 16:2 (1997): 52-62.

15. Christine L. Borgman, "Why are Online Catalogs *Still* Hard to Use?," *Journal of the American Society for Information Science* 47:7 (1996): 493-503.

16. Thomas Dowling, "The World Wide Web Meets the OPAC," *ALCTS Newsletter* 8:2 (1997): A-D.

17. Kirstie Edwards, Isabel Van Mele, Mieke Verheust, and Arthur Spaepen, "Evaluation of User Interface Design to Optimize Access to Library Databases for People Who are Motor-Impaired," *Information Technology and Libraries* 16:4 (1997): 175-180.

18. as 14. p.52.

19. Ingrid Hsieh-Yee, "Student Use of Online Catalogs and Other Information Channels," *College and Research Libraries* 57:2 (1996): 161-175.

20. Lynn Silipigni Connaway, Debra Wilcox Johnson, and Susan E. Searing, "Online Catalogs from the User's Perspective: The Use of Focus Group Interviews," *College and Research Libraries* 58:5 (1997): 403-420.

21. as 20. p.412.

22. as 14. p.56.

23. Charles R. Hildreth, "The GUI OPAC: Approach with Caution," *The Public Access Computer Systems Review* 6:5
<http://info.lib.uh.edu/pr/v6/n5/hild6n5.html>

APPENDIX 1

Date: _____

Library: _____

Web Interface: _____

SECTION 1. GENERAL OPAC DESIGN

1.1 Is a text-based interface also offered?

1.2 Are both keyword and subject heading search methods offered on the initial search page?

1.2.1 If not, is only keyword searching offered on the initial search page?

1.2.2 If not, is only subject heading searching offered on the initial search page?

1.3 Are search icons used?

1.3.1 Is the icon's meaning readily discernible independent of any accompanying text?

1.3.2 Is explanatory text contained within and/or in close proximity to the icon?

SECTION 2. KEYWORD SEARCHING

2.1 What label is used to describe keyword searching?

2.2 Is there an indication of what fields in the bibliographic record may be searched in a keyword search?

2.3 Are there instructions on how to perform a keyword search?

2.3.1 Are these instructions in close proximity to the point-of-search? ("Close proximity" defined as: instructions or clickable link to them within view as patron performs search)

2.3.2 Do instructions/HELP features incorporate conceptual aspects of searching in addition to procedures?

2.4 Are search words highlighted in retrieved bibliographic records?

2.5 Are hypertext links provided for subject headings in the bibliographic record?

2.6 For searches that retrieve at least 1 item, is help offered if the user is unsatisfied?

2.7 For searches that retrieve zero hits, are there suggestions for improving the search?

_____ Yes. OPAC prompts:

_____ No. OPAC prompts:

SECTION 3. SUBJECT HEADING SEARCHING

3.1   What label is used to describe subject heading searching?

3.2   Are users told that subject search terms must match terms from a subject list?

3.3   Are users told which subject list(s) is used in the catalog?

3.3.1 Is the subject list searchable online?

3.4   Are there instructions on how to perform a subject heading search?

3.4.1 Are these instructions in close proximity to the point-of-search?

3.4.2 Do instructions/HELP features incorporate conceptual aspects of subject heading searching in addition to procedures?

3.5   Is keyword searching of subject headings offered?

3.5.1 For keyword searches limited to subject headings that retrieve at least 1 item, is help offered if the user is unsatisfied?

3.6   Is classification number searching offered?

3.7   Are there search features that incorporate the subject heading's cross-reference structure?

3.7.1 Are "see" references hyperlinked to bibliographic records containing the correct subject heading?

3.7.2 Are there hyperlinks to bibliographic records containing broader, narrower, or related terms?

_____ BT

_____ NT

_____ RT

3.8   For searches that retrieve zero hits, are there suggestions for improving the search?

_____ Yes. OPAC prompts:

_____ No. OPAC prompts:

APPENDIX 2.
WEB-BASED OPAC SITES EVALUATED

Ameritech

1.   Omaha Public Library (NE): http://www.omaha.lib.ne.us/webpac/
2.   Richland County Public Library (SC): http://www.richland.lib.sc.us/catalog.htm
3.   Smithsonian Institute: http://www.siris.si.edu/
4.   University of Connecticut: http://www.lib.uconn.edu/homer/
5.   University of Utah: http://www.lib.utah.edu/
6.   Yale University: http://webpac.library.yale.edu/

Auto-Graphics

7.   University of Bridgeport: http://www.auto-graphics.com/cgipac/mmx/rqst

Brodart

8.   Averett College: http://www4.averett.edu/
9.   Cayuga-Onondaga School Library System (NY): http://lepac1.brodart.com/search/bq/

DRA (Data Research Associates)

10.   Austin Public Library (TX): http://www.library.ci.austin.tx.us/MARION
11.   Duke University: http://www.lib.duke.edu/online_catalog.html
12.   Fermilab (IL): http://fnlib.fnal.gov/MARION
13.   Kansas City Public Library (MO): http://web2.kcpl.lib.mo.us/
14.   Texas Christian University: http://libnt1.is.tcu.edu/opac/welcome.html
15.   University of Arkansas at Little Rock: http://libils.ualr.edu/

Endeavor

16.   American Museum of Natural History (NY): http://nimidi.amnh.org/webvoy.htm
17.   Auburn University: http://www.lib.auburn.edu/
18.   Boston Athenaeum: http://www.bostonathenaeum.org/html/webvoy.htm
19.   George Mason University: http://magik.gmu.edu/
20.   Syracuse University: http://libwww.syr.edu/summit.htm
21.   Villanova University: http://www.vill.edu/library/xfile/vucatx.htm

Gaylord

22. Boone County (OH): http://gateway.bcpl.org:4001/htbin/opac/opac_home
23. Carroll College (MT): http://corette.carroll.edu:4001/htbin/opac/opac_home

Geac

24. Boise State University: http://catalyst.idbsu.edu/
25. Pasadena Public Library (CA): http://geoweb.ci.pasadena.ca.us/

Inmagic

26. Arizona Transportation Research Center: http://www.dot.state.az.us/ABOUT/atrc/dbweb/catalog.htm
27. United States Naval Observatory: http://moon.usno.navy.mil/urania.htm

Innovative Interfaces

28. Berkeley Public Library (CA): http://library.ci.berkeley.ca.us/screens/opacmenu. html
29. Monroe County Public Library (IN): http://206.106.120.9/
30. National Institutes of Health: http://137.187.166.250/
31. Ohio State University: http://library.ohio-state.edu/search/
32. University of Colorado–Boulder: http://libraries.colorado.edu/
33. University of Oregon: http://janus.uoregon.edu/screens/opacmenu.html

Nichols Advanced Technology

34. Coeur d'Alene Public Library: http://athena.cdapl.dmi.net/
35. Piedmont Technical College (SC): http://www.piedmont.tec.sc.us/lib/lib.html

OCLC

36. University of California at Berkeley: http://sunsite.berkeley.edu:8000/

PALS

37. Creighton University: http://www.creighton.edu/PALS/

PALS (Georgia)

38. University of Georgia: http://arachnid.Gsu.EDU:8001/webpals/

SIRSI

39. Brooks Air Force Base, The Aeromedical Library (TX): http://daedalus. brooks.af.mil/
40. Lake Park Public Library (FL): http://www.coala.org:80/uhtbin/cgisirsi/ 27/60/30025
41. Noblesville-Southeastern Public Library (IN): http://webcat.nspl.lib.in. us/uhtbin/cgisirsi/93/1/1
42. University of Southern California: http://library.usc.edu/uhtbin/cgisirsi/ 0/1/1
43. University of Virginia: http://virgo.lib.virginia.edu/
44. Vanderbilt University: http://acorn.library.vanderbilt.edu/

Unknown/Home-Grown

45. Capital City Libraries (AK): http://ccl.alaska.edu/
46. Dartmouth College: http://www.dartmouth.edu/~library/
47. Indianapolis-Marion County Public Library (IN): http://www.imcpl. lib.in.us/z39.html
48. Iowa State University: http://www.lib.iastate.edu/scholar/db/icat.html
49. South Carolina Historical Society: http://www2.citadel.edu/otherserv/schs/ indexmss.html
50. Texas State Agency Libraries: http://link.tsl.state.tx.us/
51. University of California (MELVYL System): http://www.melvyl.ucop. edu/
52. University of Delaware: http://www.mis.udel.edu/webdelcat/
53. University of Texas at Austin: http://dpweb1.dp.utexas.edu/lib/utnetcat/

VTLS

54. University of Charleston (WV): http://hpk220.wvlc.wvnet.edu/virtua43/ english/
55. University of North Carolina, Charlotte: http://www1.uncc.edu:8080/ virtua/english/
56. Virginia Vocational Curriculum & Resource Center: http://vvcrc. tec.va.us/library.html
57. Westerville Public Library (OH): http://www.wpl.lib.oh.us/vtls/english/

WebLUIS

58. Florida State University: http://webluis.fcla.edu/cgi-bin/cgiwrap/fclwlui/ webluis

WebPALS (Minnesota)

59. All Minnesota libraries: http://www.pals.msus.edu/webpals/home.html

WebPALS (South Dakota)

60. All South Dakota libraries: http://webpals.sdln.net/

NB: Full data for each site surveyed may be obtained from the author or the editors.

The Internet as a Tool for Cataloguing and Classification, a View from the UK

Gordon Dunsire

SUMMARY. The use of various Internet services by library cataloguers and subject classifiers is discussed, with special reference to Scotland and the remainder of the United Kingdom. Services include e-mail,
FTP, and Websites. *[Article copies available for a fee from The Haworth Document Delivery Service: 1-800-342-9678. E-mail address: getinfo@haworthpressinc.
com <Website: http://www.haworthpressinc.com>]*

KEYWORDS. Libraries, cataloguing, classification, subject analysis,
Internet, World Wide Web

The Internet provides facilities for peer-to-peer and broadcast communication using e-mail, online publication and dissemination of professional and technical literature using HTML and FTP technologies,
and global access to systems, services and resources originally designed for access by restricted sets of users. All of these facilities can
be used to develop and improve the process of cataloguing, classification, and indexing, and have been taken up by many professional
cataloguers and information managers who have ready access to the
Internet.

Gordon Dunsire is Sub-Librarian, Information Strategy & IT Development,
Library, Napier University, Edinburgh EH11 4BN, Scotland (g.dunsire@napier.
ac.uk).

[Haworth co-indexing entry note]: "The Internet as a Tool for Cataloguing and Classification, a View
from the UK." Dunsire, Gordon. Co-published simultaneously in *Journal of Internet Cataloging* (The
Haworth Information Press, an imprint of The Haworth Press, Inc.) Vol. 2, No. 3/4, 2000, pp. 187-195;
and: *Internet Searching and Indexing: The Subject Approach* (ed: Alan R. Thomas, and James R. Shearer)
The Haworth Information Press, an imprint of The Haworth Press, Inc., 2000, pp. 187-195. Single or multiple
copies of this article are available for a fee from The Haworth Document Delivery Service [1-800-342-9678,
9:00 a.m. - 5:00 p.m. (EST). E-mail address: getinfo@haworthpressinc.com].

187

Easy access to the Internet in the UK has been enjoyed by librarians working in higher education and commercial libraries for a number of years. However, it is only since 1998 that most schools, further education colleges, and public libraries have been able to get connected as a result of Government initiatives such as the National Grid for Learning,[1] the People's Network,[2] and the University for Industry.[3] Much of the evolution of the use of the Internet as a tool for cataloguing has therefore been driven by the needs and working practices of the university and research library community, and a significant part of the infrastructure is still funded and managed through the aegis of the regional Higher Education Funding Councils and subject-based Research Councils. However, access to this infrastructure by non-academic users is increasing, not least because of a broadening of the definition of education and research as applied to resources and users.

Professional discussion using e-mail is facilitated by the Mailbase[4] service based at the University of Newcastle. Mailbase allows anyone in the UK higher education community to set up an electronic discussion list or listserve. It is funded by the Joint Information Systems Committee (JISC),[5] and is free at point of use. The service currently hosts nearly 2500 different discussion lists with a total membership of nearly 170,000 participants. Several lists are concerned with issues of cataloguing and classification; most, but not all, used the standard prefix lis (for library and information services, not 'list') as part of their name. Lis-ukmarc[6] is concerned with the harmonisation of the American, British and Canadian MARC formats, and general issues for UKMARC. Lis-cigs[7] is used by the Cataloguing and Indexing Group in Scotland, a branch of the Library Association's Cataloguing and Indexing Group, to discuss the cataloguing and classification of electronic information resources ranging from CD-ROMs to Websites, as well as general Group business. A number of Web pages are attached to this list, giving examples of the application of UKMARC to cataloguing electronic journals, notes from seminars and workshops, and links to related resources. Other lists, such as lis-serials,[8] focus on library operations, including cataloguing, for specific categories of material. New approaches to information retrieval are also represented at Mailbase; there is a suite of lists discussing various aspects of the Dublin Core proposals for metadata, the broadest of which is dc-general.[9] Most of these lists are open; anyone can join or send messages, and membership is not restricted to UK librarians.

Peer-to-peer communication with cataloguers working in Scotland is assisted, to a certain extent, by SLAINTE[10] (Scottish Libraries Across the Internet), a Website run jointly by the Scottish Library Association and Scottish Library and Information Council. This includes a directory of nearly all library and information services in all sectors in Scotland, with postal and e-mail addresses, telephone and fax numbers, and organisational URLs. Although specific information about cataloguers is sparse, SLAINTE can be useful as a starting point for making contact. There are no cross-sectoral directories of library personnel working in the rest of the UK, and there is no single source of information, online or otherwise, containing comprehensive details of cataloguers or subject classifiers working in the UK.

Useful material on catalogue and subject standards is made accessible on Websites managed by the agencies responsible for maintaining and developing those standards. Information about the UKMARC standard is published on a Website managed by the British Library National Bibliographic Service.[11] The bulk of the material is concerned with the ongoing MARC harmonisation process and changes to the standard. An online summary of UKMARC tags and subfields and a draft of the UNIMARC classification format are available; both have some use as quick-reference tools but lack internal navigational or searching facilities. The USMARC Website[12] managed by the Library of Congress Network Development and MARC Standards Office contains more information. Much of this is of interest to UKMARC users, including lists of codes for geographical areas and languages which have already been harmonised, and documentation on tags and subfields where harmonisation is likely to be agreed. Many British libraries have already adopted, or plan to migrate to, USMARC. Cataloguers can make themselves better informed about the issues surrounding the development and evolution of these standards, and plan more effectively the implementation of required changes at a local level.

Other official Websites of relevance include those of the Joint Steering Committee for Revision of Anglo-American Cataloguing Rules (AACR),[13] and the International Federation of Library Associations and Institutions (IFLA). AACR is undergoing significant development to accommodate new electronic media and bring it into closer line with other international standards; the Website publishes records of discussion and papers arising from these activities. A current focus involves integrating AACR with ISBD(ER), the International Standard Bibliographic Description for Electronic Resources, a standard maintained by IFLA. IFLA provides information on its Website about the work of its Division of Bibliographic Control,[14] and its Section on Cataloguing[15] including the full text of ISBD(ER).

Information about standards for subject analysis and classification can be found in another area of the IFLA Website devoted to its Section on Classification and Indexing.[16] Websites are also available for the two major classification schemes used by most libraries: the Dewey Decimal Classification (DDC),[17] and the Library of Congress Classification (LC).[18] Both sites publish summaries of the classification schedules and lists of new topics and notations. Neither site offers a complete online version of their schemes–indeed, the range of publications and other information made freely available in electronic versions is less than that available in print. Several factors are probably involved. Many of the Websites are less than a couple of years old, and time and staff resources may be insufficient to retrospectively publish older, print-based material. The production of documentation on standards, manuals, and conference proceedings has been used as an informal indicator of organisational effectiveness, which can be less easy to interpret in terms of Web 'pages' and 'hits.' Much of this material has been sold to end-users in the past, and financial managers may be reluctant to reduce or stop income-generating activities, even if little profit is actually involved. However, a lot of newly-created material is being published online, and is free because production costs have been absorbed during the creation of the print version. E-mail archives and notes of conference proceedings ensure that current issues are disseminated electronically. With many standards under active development, new online versions will gradually replace off-line printed documents, even where there are no plans to digitise and retroconvert. It seems reasonable to expect, then, that cataloguers and classifiers will soon be able to call up displays of comprehensive, up-to-date codes of practice, schedules, rules, and other reference sources online and when they require them. Some organisations will also seek to recoup costs by imposing some form of charging for such information, particularly if further investment is required to develop more appropriate interfaces, for example to support searching, retrieval, and downloading to local systems. Decisions will need to take into account organisational goals, funding streams, loss of income as print-based activities are reduced, costs of maintaining information online, and value perceived by the end-user.

The supply of bibliographic records via electronic media has been developing for much longer. In the UK, the first system for the national distribution of catalogue records in UKMARC format was created by the British Library (BL) in the late 1970s, in the form of LOCAS (Local Cataloguing Service). Today, the BL is one of several organisations providing Internet access to records, not only those created by BL but also records from other sources such as the Library of Congress, in both UKMARC and USMARC formats. Commercial services provide facilities for searching and downloading MARC records created by cataloguing co-operatives and consortia, for example SLS (Information Systems) Ltd sells records from the Research Libraries Group[19] as well as from the ubiquitous BL and LC sources. There is intense competition in retailing bibliographic data and prices have been dropping for downloading records. Ameritech Library Services (UK) Ltd reduced its per-record charge from 35p to 20p, at the same time as abolishing an annual subscription fee of £1000.[20] Interface software is often supplied free of charge, such as SLS's Z39.50 browser, and there may be no fee for just viewing a record on screen. Indeed, records from the national cataloguing agencies, such as the BL and LC, may eventually enter the public domain completely. The BL License for using its MARC records is free to most libraries, and allows them to exchange BL records freely for non-commercial purposes.

One of the most significant benefits of the Internet for cataloguers and classifiers is for day-to-day intellectual and professional support. Strategic planning and operations development is catered for by the resources and services already mentioned. The Internet gives immediate access to millions of records created by professionals with a great deal of expertise and experience in applying complex standards to materials which have been examined in the context of large or specialised collections. Cataloguers with less experience or limited opportunity to make decisions requiring contextual analysis can avail themselves of the work already done. In particular, problems of uniform titles, the authoritative forms of personal and corporate names, subject analysis, and the application of standard classification schemes, can often be confidently and quickly resolved by checking catalogue records created in larger libraries. Uniform titles need to be determined on the basis of all versions of the specific work; name authority forms are usually based on the version prevalent across all of the person's or organisation's output. Both can be extremely difficult to ascertain if the cataloguer does not have access to sufficiently large collections. Cataloguers can use the Internet to connect to the catalogues of very large libraries or groups of libraries, and utilise their internal search and retrieve interfaces, or exploit Z39.50 (an international standard protocol for searching and retrieving data) to use the local interface to interrogate many other catalogue systems. The cataloguer can then see how similar works have been catalogued, and may be lucky enough to find an existing record for the work in hand, copyright and licensing permitting.

Problems in subject analysis and classification can also be resolved by recourse to greater expertise. Subject headings and classification numbers added by subject experts to records for similar works can be used to establish the correct form of heading or number at the local level. Some care may be required to determine which standards have been used, for example the edition of DDC applied and whether LC Subject Headings or BL PRECIS (now defunct) is the source of the subject vocabulary. Other problems lie with identifying local embellishments to standards, and the use of options within standard schemes. In order to use subject-based searching as effectively as possible, cataloguers also need to be aware of how indexes on the host system are implemented, including the use of stop words, synonyms and thesauri. It can be difficult to find the DDC number for a subject if there is only a classified index for subject retrieval. Nonetheless, the cataloguer with limited knowledge can often find sufficient clues in other bibliographic records to correctly identify the subject of the work in hand and apply a local classification or heading to it.

Collections of online catalogues are available on many Websites. Lists of URLs for Web-based catalogues or WebCats arranged by geographical area, library type and system vendor, can be found on a Canadian site maintained by Peter Scott.[21] Each catalogue has to be searched separately, using different search protocols and interfaces, and manual co-ordination of records retrieved from more than one host is required. Since 1998, the UK's Electronic Libraries programme, eLib,[22] has been funding the development of Z39.50 for broadcast searching of multiple library catalogues and consolidation of retrieved records. This takes the form of a number of 'clumps' projects,[23] including CAIRNS[24] which includes all of the Scottish universities and several major public libraries. These projects have already identified several relevant issues, including the need to define collection coverage and local indexing schema so that the user can better choose which catalogues to search. The projects have also highlighted areas where divergence of standards is greater than might have been expected. Retrieval by subject is particularly poor, and users need to know what is being mapped to the subject indexes, what local interpretations of standards have been made, and how consistently the current standards have been applied across the catalogue, before estimating how accurate the results of a particular search will be.

Traugott Koch gives a plethora of different subject vocabularies, in the context of Dublin Core, in a section of the Nordic DC Metadata Creator Website;[25] the list of sources is arranged in subject order following the main classes of DDC. The problems of semantic interoperability between different vocabularies and categorisation schemes have been understood by library classifiers for many years, but there was little perceived need to co-ordinate or standardise until the evolution of technologies for connecting many different catalogues to non-local enquirers. The issue has now, in a short space of time, become acute, and is adversely affecting the benefits of resource sharing, collection management, and information retrieval which should accrue from wide-area networking. There seems little hope for much progress. Indeed, the process of developing new standards for the creation and use of metadata, such as Dublin Core, is paying as little attention to subject retrieval as that paid by traditional cataloguers. The interchange and migration of data between different formats is less of a problem, and several conversion tools are currently freely available on some websites. For example, different types of MARC format can be converted using UseMARCON,[26] while the Logos Library System offers a MARC to XML to MARC convertor.[27]

The Internet, then, is a powerful tool for assisting cataloguers with their work, facilitating the evolution and development of cataloguing standards, and, ironically, exposing the shortcomings of existing practices. If a trained, professional library cataloguer finds it difficult to retrieve information from someone else's catalogue, how many library users, without the benefit of esoteric knowledge, are finding it frustrating to use the cataloguer's local system? At the same time, the Internet provides an infrastructure for alleviating or resolving some of these problems, and for developing better services for all users of information.

NOTES

1. *National Grid for Learning*
<URL: http://www.dfee.gov.uk/grid/index.htm> Seen 29 Jul 1999.
   2. *New library: The people's network*
<URL: http://www.ukoln.ac.uk/services/lic/newlibrary/> Seen 29 Jul 1999.
   3. *University for Industry: Engaging people in learning for life*
<URL: http://www.dfee.gov.uk/ufi/index.htm> Seen 29 Jul 1999.
   4. *Mailbase*
<URL: http://www.mailbase.ac.uk/> (20 Jul 1999) Seen 29 Jul 1999.
   5. *Joint Information Systems Committee: Networks and innovative services for higher education*
<URL: http://www.jisc.ac.uk/> (22 Apr 1999) Seen 29 Jul 1999.
   6. *lis-ukmarc*
<URL: http://www.mailbase.ac.uk/lists/lis-ukmarc/> (2 Jul 1999) Seen 29 Jul 1999.
   7. *lis-cigs*
<URL: http://www.mailbase.ac.uk/lists/lis-cigs/> (24 Jun 1999) Seen 29 Jul 1999.
   8. *lis-serials*
<URL: http://www.mailbase.ac.uk/lists/lis-serials/> (26 Jul 1999) Seen 29 Jul 1999.
   9. *dc-general*
<URL: http://www.mailbase.ac.uk/lists/dc-general/> (29 Jul 1999) Seen 29 Jul 1999.
   10. *SLAINTE: Scottish libraries across the Internet*
<URL: http://www.slainte.org.uk/> (26 May 1999) Seen 29 Jul 1999.
   11. *UKMARC web page*
<URL: http://www.bl.uk/services/bsds/nbs/marc/> Seen 29 Jul 1999.
   12. *MARC standards*
<URL: http://lcweb.loc.gov/marc/> (24 Jun 1999) Seen 29 Jul 1999.
   13. *Joint Steering Committee for Revision of Anglo-American Cataloguing Rules*
<URL: http://www.nlc-bnc.ca/jsc/> Seen 29 Jul 1999.
   14. *International Federation of Library Associations and Institutions: Division of Bibliographic Control*
<URL: http://www.ifla.org/VII/d4/dbc.htm> (18 Feb 1999) Seen 29 Jul 1999.
   15. *International Federation of Library Associations and Institutions: Section on Cataloguing*
<URL: http://www.ifla.org/VII/s13/sc.htm> (2 Feb 1999) Seen 29 Jul 1999.
   16. *International Federation of Library Associations and Institutions: Section on Classification and Indexing*
<URL: http://www.ifla.org/VII/s29/sci.htm> (1 Mar 1999) Seen 29 Jul 1999.
   17. *Dewey Decimal Classification*
<URL: http://www.oclc.org/fp/> (26 Jul 1999) Seen 29 Jul 1999.
   18. *The Library of Congress Cataloging Policy & Support Office. Library of Congress Classification*
<URL: http://lcweb.loc.gov/catdir/cpso/cpso.html#class> (21 Jul 1999) Seen 29 Jul 1999.
   19. *Research Libraries Group site directory*
<URL: http://www.thames.rlg.org/toc.html> (16 Jul 1999) Seen 29 Jul 1999.

20. "Cost of BNB & LC records plummets to 20p per record," *D-mail* 6:2 (May 1999).

21. *Monster crawler: Search all the major search engines with just one click!* <URL: http://www.lights.com/webcats/> Seen 29 Jul 1999.

22. *elib: Electronic Libraries programme*
<URL: http://www.ukoln.ac.uk/services/elib/> (29 Jul 1999) Seen 29 Jul 1999.

23. *Clump projects dissemination activities*
<URL: http://www.shef.ac.uk/~riding/docs/dissemal.html> (1 Apr 1999) Seen 29 Jul 1999.

24. *CAIRNS: Co-operative Academic Information Retrieval Network for Scotland*
<URL: http://cairns.lib.gla.ac.uk/> (27 Jul 1999) Seen 29 Jul 1999.

25. *DC Subject. Thesauri and classification systems available in the WWW*
<URL: http://www.ub.lu.se/metadata/subject-help.html> (3 May 1999) Seen 29 Jul 1999.

26. *UseMARCON: User controlled generic MARC convertor*
<URL: http://www.konbib.nl/kb/sbo/bibinfra/usema-en.htm> Seen 29 Jul 1999.

27. *MARC XML*
<URL: http://www.logos.com/marc/marcxml.htm> (9 Nov 1998) Seen 29 Jul 1999.

USE, the Universal Subject Environment: A New Subject Access Approach in the Time of the Internet

William E. Studwell

SUMMARY. USE, a new subject approach particularly designed for automated use on the Internet and elsewhere, is proposed. This system combines a fixed linguistic component with a simple and consistent structure for combination of terms, suitable for multinational, multicultural and multilingual use. Examples of its use in practice are given. An international implementation approach for USE is provided. *[Article copies available for a fee from The Haworth Document Delivery Service: 1-800-342-9678. E-mail address: getinfo@haworthpressinc.com <Website: http:// www.haworthpressinc.com>]*

KEYWORDS. USE (Universal Subject Environment), Internet, Library of Congress Subject Headings, vocabulary control, string indexing

TWO MAJOR PROBLEMS CONVERGE

With the blossoming in the 1990s of the Information Superhighway–the World Wide Web, or the Internet–the sector of the library and

William E. Studwell is Principal Cataloger and Professor, University Libraries, Northern Illinois University, DeKalb, Illinois 60115-2868 (c60wes1@wpo.cso.niu.edu).

[Haworth co-indexing entry note]: "USE, the Universal Subject Environment: A New Subject Access Approach in the Time of the Internet." Studwell, William E. Co-published simultaneously in *Journal of Internet Cataloging* (The Haworth Information Press, an imprint of The Haworth Press, Inc) Vol. 2, No. 3/4, 2000, pp. 197-209; and: *Internet Searching and Indexing: The Subject Approach* (ed: Alan R. Thomas, and James R. Shearer) The Haworth Information Press, an imprint of The Haworth Press, Inc., 2000, pp. 197-209. Single or multiple copies of this article are available for a fee from The Haworth Document Delivery Service [1-800-342-9678, 9:00 a.m. - 5:00 p.m. (EST). E-mail address: getinfo@haworthpressinc.com].

information community charged with cataloging, establishing biblio-graphic control of, or "managing"[1] information resources has one additional major concern with which to deal. The Internet, which in a real and everyday way is an electronic replication of the activity of the world in general, has thus provided yet another area for debate and decision-making for catalogers. Although *whether* to even bother cata-loging Internet resources is a topic not firmly resolved,[2] the general consensus seems to be that selective bibliographic control of the Inter-net is not only desirable but necessary.[3] While *which* Internet re-sources to catalog is an acquisitions or collection development deci-sion, similar to decisions made for books, microforms, films, computer files, and other materials, *how* to catalog information found on the Internet is among the responsibilities of the cataloging commu-nity.

This view is reinforced by recent efforts to develop international standards for cataloging material on the Internet, as reflected in two 1996 articles by Jean Weihs. One essay[4] described the bibliographic difficulties of the Internet, and the other[5] was a call for input to aid the formulation of Internet cataloging standards. At this point it is not certain that the standards that eventually will be developed will in-clude any concrete or substantial proposals for subject access to the Internet. Most likely, that controversial topic will either be bypassed or remain unresolved. Although there have been several general codifica-tions or major modifications of descriptive cataloging in recent de-cades,[6] and there is a current movement to once again modify descrip-tive cataloging,[7] there have been no international standards for linguistic subject access to information, or at least none that have been widely disseminated.

That is, there is really no world-wide functional system using lan-guage, other than keyword searching, search engines, and other elec-tronic methodologies, to help find material on the Internet or on li-brary shelves. The extensive comprehensive listing of subject terms, accompanied by various linking references, which is produced by the Library of Congress is used in many nations, but is only in the loosest interpretation a true or easily-describable system. Many improvements have been made to LCSH (Library of Congress Subject Headings) in the past decade and a half, but there is still no published or known complete set of theoretical or philosophical principles to serve as a fundamental document for creation and utilization of these headings.

Some basic principles have been suggested in the past, for example, by Julia Pettee,[8] and David Haykin,[9] while LC's Subject Cataloging Manual[10] includes some broad general principles in its various editions, particularly from the 1985 revision. In 1991, some significant steps toward the goal of codification of LCSH, that is, producing a comprehensive rule book, were made at a seminar sponsored by the Library of Congress,[11] but there has not been any visible progress since then. This conference was convened largely in response to what was described as the "subject code" movement. That 1980s-early 1990s phenomenon perhaps started as early as Sanford Berman's 1979 rudimentary proposal for a subject heading code for public, school and community college libraries,[12] although Lois Chan[13] amongst others had previously made comments about the need for a subject heading code for LCSH.

The main fuel for the subject code movement, however, was provided by the present author in his 1985 essay "Why Not an 'AACR' for Subject Headings?"[6] followed up by a variety of other writings putting forth a large number of specific proposals to help in the development of a theoretical code. These publications included a book comprehensively outlining relevant philosophical principles.[14] One of the signs of the ending of the movement, or at least that phase of it, was Studwell's 1994 essay, "Who Killed the Subject Code?"[15] which examined the issues associated with the apparent demise of the code movement. Yet concern with problems of LCSH did not cease with that 1994 essay which did, despite its title, suggest the issue was far from dead. Thus, in 1995 Lisa Romero,[16] speaking from the viewpoint of a library science student, commented on the lack of any theoretical or philosophical principles for the development and assignment of LCSH, and on the adverse effects of this shortcoming on library education. In 1996, Tschera Harkness Connell,[17] speaking from the viewpoint of an everyday cataloging practitioner, observed from her research that academic libraries were not keeping up with the numerous changes to LCSH in recent years. In 1997, Thomas Mann[18] of the Library of Congress noted that debate continues in library schools over whether LCSH are still useful and viable as tools for information access. And in the same year Studwell, in response to Connell, stated that the failure of academic libraries to keep pace with the steady barrage of LCSH changes was not primarily due to budgetary or philosophical factors but "the reality that LC seems to be operating without any kind of plan or guiding principles."[19]

In spite of this absence of a long term strategy or a standardization code, LCSH remain the world's most heavily-used single list of controlled vocabulary terms for subject access. Some form of LCSH usage can be found in a variety of countries, including some nations which are not predominantly English-speaking. Although there have been a variety of claims that LCSH or other subject heading systems are redundant in the new environment of electronic information systems, a number of studies have indicated that some type of established terminology is needed to provide maximal subject retrieval using OPACs. Notable among these studies are those of James Dwyer[20] and Joan Cherry.[21] Since these studies were published in 1987 and 1992, that is, relatively early in the debate over the continued viability of controlled vocabularies such as LCSH, and have yet to be contradicted by later studies, the issue of using a controlled vocabulary to access materials by subject, complementing various computerized methodologies, should be a dead one. Yet Sanford Berman considered necessary a reiteration of the need for controlled vocabulary as late as 1998 when he observed:

> Without controlled, contemporary, cross-referenced subject headings that are generously and consistently assigned, there's no assurance whatever that a mere "keyword" search will actually identify all relevant works in a collection or database.[22]

In summary, the failure of the Library of Congress to develop a comprehensive theoretical subject heading code on which to base a subject access system for the future appears not to be a dead issue. It remains a major unresolved problem, number one of two interdependent issues. The lack of general cataloging standards for the Internet is problem number two. Therefore, the task of creating guidelines for cataloging Internet resources is obstructed by these two converging major problems.

THE PROPOSAL

These obstacles, however, can be overcome. Presuming that standards for descriptive cataloging will be successfully assembled within the next several years, standards for subject cataloging can also be achieved by codifying LCSH and modifying individual headings to match the standards. If this task turns out to be insurmountable because of the lack of cooperation by the Library of Congress for financial, staffing, or philosophical reasons, then a substitute system using many of the same concepts could be developed. Linguistic subject access to Internet resources does not require a different type of system than is required for books, maps, sound recordings, images, serials, and other long-established fountains of information. Although some specific form subdivisions for Internet resources, such as "–Internet resources" or "–Internet catalogs," may need to be established, there is no fundamental difference between the controlled vocabulary needed for Internet resources and that needed for other sources of information. As noted above, the Internet is to a large extent an electronic mirror of the rest of human activity, and any controlled subject vocabulary developed to access the Internet should mirror the vocabulary used for the remainder of our existence.

The Internet is a world-wide system, encompassing most if not all nations, cultures, and languages. A recent issue of *Communications,* the monthly journal of the Association for Computing Machinery, sporting the bold title "Digital Libraries: Global Scope, Unlimited Access,"[23] clearly reinforced the global reach and impact of current information technologies. Therefore, the fixed linguistic component devised to provide subject access to the Internet should also be both logically and practically multinational, multicultural, and multilingual in scope. "Fixed linguistic component" is this author's phrase for a controlled and well-organized comprehensive set of subject terms which contrasts with random linguistic subject access by automatic digital means. The various electronic methodologies such as keyword searching and search engines that would complement and supplement any controlled vocabulary already transcend national, cultural, and linguistic boundaries. If LCSH or a substitute entity of similar pattern or design are adopted for the Internet, such a tool would almost of necessity have to be Multinational, Multicultural, and Multilingual. This author first proposed this "3M" concept in a short essay in 1998.[24]

The concept was expanded in a subsequent article.[25] Designated the "Universal Subject Environment" ("USE"), the new subject access system would combine a controlled vocabulary with other available techniques for subject retrieval via computer. There is a difference between the present mixes of controlled vocabulary and computerized methodology and the proposed USE. This difference is that the fixed linguistic component (controlled vocabulary) of USE would be considerably dissimilar from present LCSH although quite possibly being a major adaptation of LCSH.

The fixed linguistic component of USE would have to be simple, consistent, and clear in structure, language, and relationships to fulfill its goal to be multinational, multicultural, and multilingual. There could be no structural irregularities, no inversions, no confusing exceptions, no adjectives except when unavoidable, no clumsy phrases (such as those using "and" or "in"), no other linguistic complications such as declensions and prescribed order of terms. Just one of the patterns currently a part of LCSH, "Short stories, Chinese," "Short stories, French," etc., exemplifies several of these difficulties. "Short stories, Chinese" is an inversion, a structural irregularity or exception to the topically-similar pattern "Chinese fiction," and unnecessarily uses an adjective. Two other patterns, "Parent and child" and "Dogs in art" are examples of both awkward phrases and prescribed order of terms. There would also be improved relational punctuation. All this will facilitate multinationalism, multiculturalism, and translation from one language to another. Even if one language, such as English, becomes the primary or predominant language for linguistic international information exchange, thus making the multilingual aspect of USE more or less moot, the simplicity, clarity, and consistency of USE will facilitate usage by those who have learned the predominant language as a second language.

THE THEORY BEHIND THE FIXED LINGUISTIC COMPONENT

The theoretical foundations of USE, as outlined in the 1998[25] essay, are now developed here with several additions and other modifications. Improved structure and accompanying improved punctuation are the main ingredients of the proposed design. Single word terms would always be preferred, and a three element punctuation system would be implemented. The punctuation system employs the

- dash–to represent a subordinate relationship
- equals sign = to represent an equivalence relationship
- slash / to represent any other relationships between terms.

It should be noted here that these punctuation marks are used in some other schemes, such as the Universal Decimal Classification, but with different significance.

The dash, as in current LCSH practice, would imply subordination of successive elements, for example:

History–Philosophy–Bibliography

Philosophy–History–Bibliography

The first example means a bibliography of works on the philosophy of history, while in contrast, the second example would mean a bibliography on the history of philosophy. Proper order is necessary in the usage of the dash. A possible alternative to the dash might be a colon, though this is used with different meaning in the Universal Decimal Classification and other schemes.

The second punctuation component, the equals sign, new to LCSH, would be used only for groups of persons and would imply different personal facets or traits, for example:

Women=Lawyers

Women=Lawyers=Chinese

The first example means women who are lawyers and the second example means women who are Chinese in nationality and who are also lawyers. The term "Chinese" by itself would necessarily mean the group of people because "Chinese" would not stand alone in relation to language and literature. Order of elements in this type of structure is unimportant since this scheme is to be used in automated systems. The second example could just as well be "Lawyers=Chinese= Women," "Lawyers=Women=Chinese," "Chinese=Women= Lawyers," "Chinese=Lawyers=Women," or "Women=Chinese=Lawyers." As long as there is some type of prescribed marker, like the x, y, and z currently used in MARC coding of LCSH, that the computer can read and correctly interpret between each and every usage of punctuation, access would be easy and reliable no matter how the heading is assembled. For the "Women=Lawyers=Chinese" example above, the search could use any or all of these three terms in any order and achieve retrieval. In this type of situation and all other patterns proposed in USE, the precision, simplicity, clarity, and control inherent in USE will provide more reliable retrieval than is presently the case for LCSH.

The third element of punctuation, also new to LCSH but used in other schemes, would be the slash. It would imply any type of relationship other than the equals relationship between two or more groups of persons and the subordination relationship indicated by dashes. For example, a work on the relationship between women and lawyers would be "Women/Lawyers." Also, a work on the relationship between children and parents would be "Children/Parents." Again, order would not be important. Slashes would have a huge variety of potential usage, including: "Statistics/Physics" or "Physics/Statistics" instead of "Statistical physics," for a work on statistical methods used in physics, as compared to a collection of statistics about physics which would be represented by "Physics–Statistics"; "Illinois/Poetry" or "Poetry/Illinois" for a work discussing the theme of the midwestern state as used in poetry; "Spirit/Life" or "Life/Spirit" for a work on spiritual life; and "China/Art–Bibliography" for a bibliography on the theme of that country in works of art. "China/Art" or "Art/China" would also mean any relationship between China and Art other than the art work produced in China, which is represented by "Art–China." Since "China/Art" or "Art/China" has no geographical subdivision punctuation, it cannot mean the art of China. Although different from what we are used to, the proposed punctuation system has a strong logical foundation.

All three elements would be used together in any order except for the subordination pattern inherent to the slash punctuation. Some examples of themes and their USE representation are as follows.

Theme	USE Representation
Calcium physiology in humans	Humans–Physiology/Calcium
The physiology of tobacco in Americans	Tobacco/Americans–Physiology
The history of Italian-Americans	Italians=Americans–History
Drug abuse as it affects Mexican-U.S. relations	
	Mexico–Relations–United States/Drugs/Abuse
Economics relating to the education of French-Canadian librarians	
	French=Canadians=Librarians–Education/Economics
Sports injuries in aged women	Women=Aged/Sports–Injuries

These strings of terms are not particularly complex, and any portion of them would readily be extracted in a variety of searches. Note that the strings are given above in a left to right pattern, but could just as easily be written right to left.

The slash would also be used to handle usages of the same term in different disciplines in lieu of using parenthetical qualifiers. For example, the word vague "interest" would be accommodated as follows.

USE representation	*Interpretation*
Interest/Money	earnings on funds
Interest/Investments	a holding in stocks or other investments
Interest/Psychology	mental attention to something
Interest/Money/Psychology	mental attention to earnings on funds
Interest/Money/Islam/Law	Islamic law relating to earnings on funds

Again, this structure, with markers accompanying each use of punctuation, would allow for easy retrieval by any of the elements provided or by any combination of elements.

Using the three types of punctuation with their distinct connotations would provide an almost infinite flexibility in heading creation and in subject retrieval with less sacrifice of overall clarity than is presently the case for LCSH. The above examples are only indications of what might be done with the USE approach, and not necessarily final realities. The overall simple design, not the proposed details, is the key. A big bonus to this type of structure is that such terms would in most cases be convertible from one language to another, recognizing that machine translators will have to accommodate terms which are not exact one-to-one equivalents.

Perhaps the major problem in such a structural and punctuation arrangement would be those multiple word topical terms not conducive to conversion to two or more noun terms. (Names of places, persons, and organizations would, of course, remain in their present forms.) While the concept of American literature is easily convertible to "Literature–United States," Chinese literature to "Literature–China," and Russian-American literature to "Literature–United States/Russia," various terms for scientific, technical, historical, and cultural concepts are not readily convertible and would be left in their natural language forms. These necessary exemptions could include "Calcium chloride" (which is not the same as another heading "Calcium/Chlorides"), "Red squirrels," "Black holes," and "World War II, 1939-1945." Note that the multiple concept "Red squirrels" may well be accommodated by the term combination "Squirrels–Red," but the single concept "Black holes" cannot really be accommodated by the term combination "Holes–Black."

Using the above principles, complemented by a comprehensive and reliable reference system that will lead the user from "American literature" to "Literature–United States," from "Spiritual life" to "Spirit/ Life" or "Life/Spirit," and so on, the result would be a linguistic system that is considerably easier to use than the current haphazard and inconsistent LCSH listing, the irregularities of which have been noted above. The clarity, simplicity, and logic of the proposed USE system would replace the present LCSH system which relies on a very good memory or frequent searching of the present four volume LCSH printed listing or the equivalent in electronic form. While LCSH is a poorly-organized listing of allowable terms, USE is a much simpler and more precise listing of allowable terms along with rules for their combination. USE by design would neither list nor prohibit any specific combinations. It would be in the long-range interest of the Library of Congress to support the USE system since it perpetuates their concepts of precoordinated terminology and controlled vocabulary, albeit in an evolutionary modified form. A failure by the Library of Congress to work towards the development of USE or a similar scheme could eventually lead to the demise of LCSH and create major difficulties for present users of these headings who may have to adopt a very different subject access method. In addition, it should be noted that library education in the future would be facilitated by studying USE with its logical simplicity.

When the proposed system as described above or in another design is accepted on an international basis, the Library of Congress and other cataloging agencies would continue to supply pre-established terms for subject access. If the Library of Congress, for example, supplies the heading Literature–United States–19th century–History/ Criticism, meaning both history of and analysis of 19th century American literature, French-speaking areas can easily convert it to Littérature–États-Unis–19e siècle–Histoire/Critique. Similarly, conversions to languages without alphabets such as Chinese, or languages with situational grammatical shifts such as Russian, would be facilitated by the simplicity of USE.

IMPLEMENTATION OF USE

The proposed Universal Subject Environment would be as useful and effective for print and audiovisual materials as for the Internet. The implementation of USE for material on the Internet suggests usage of search engines, possibly one or more specifically designed for USE. No matter what types of information it may help to retrieve, USE would serve as the general subject access strategy for the future. Something similar to USE is probably in the future of library and information science even if this particular system is not adopted. The process for implementation of USE or a related system would probably be to start with the International Federation of Library Associations, specifically their Committee on Cataloguing. National libraries from important countries, for example, the Library of Congress and the British Library, plus important national professional associations, for example, the American Library Association in the U.S. and the Library Association in Britain, would collectively or separately bring the USE proposal to IFLA. The Library of Congress, as discussed above, may hesitate or even refuse to petition for the adoption of USE since the new strategy would involve the replacement of their present controlled vocabulary by another. But because USE would in reality perpetuate the patterns of subject headings created by the Library of Congress, and because there will probably be some kind of future pre-established subject terminology utilized for the Internet as well as for other venues, support of USE or a variant by the Library of Congress would in effect be an affirmation of their past major contributions to subject access and their commitment to the future.

Presuming that IFLA would support USE or a variant, they would first select a multinational, multicultural, and multilingual committee including representatives from the major national libraries, professional library and information associations, and other interested groups throughout the world. That committee would work out the details of the controlled vocabulary and its supporting computer methodologies, and, it is hoped, do it in a reasonable period of time. After a draft or prototype version is completed, pilot studies should be carried out, with international feedback geared toward further development. If the new system is kept simple and the goal of a truly global product is kept firmly in mind by all participants, the achievement of the agreement on the theoretical and practical aspects of the new system is quite feasible. It seems as if just about everything else of wide scale significance is becoming global, so it is not unreasonable for subject access to join the ever expanding club of international cooperation.

Publicity and marketing would follow. To implement USE after the theoretical principles and technical standards are agreed upon, a broad-based group of agencies and organizations throughout the world would be expected to embrace and promote it. These groups could be expected to include national professional associations, national libraries, relevant governmental agencies, commercial companies, and library and information science schools.

If effective in subject retrieval, reasonable in cost, and international in scope, USE will work well for its initial users. Those groups and organizations who choose to reject or delay their active participation in USE will find themselves deprived of a valuable modern tool.

NOTES

1. Note this usage of the vague term "managing" which has been recently used as a substitute term for "cataloging" or "bibliographic control," thus raising some professional disquiet in anticipation of a possible shift in attitude away from disciplined and rigorous bibliographic control. William E. Studwell, "No More Ducks in a Row: An Internet Loss", *Technicalities* 17:2 (1997): 3, 5.

2. William E. Studwell, "Are Catalogers Ready for the Information Superhighway?", *Technicalities* 14:7 (1994): 2-3.

3. William E. Studwell, "Logging on and Cata-logging: Some Thoughts on Bibliographical Control of the Internet", *Behavioral and Social Sciences Librarian* 16:1 (1997): 69-71.

4. Jean Weihs, "Interfaces: Solving the Internet Nightmare", *Technicalities* 16:4 (1996): 4-6.

5. Jean Weihs, "Interfaces: A Call to Arms", *Technicalities* 16:6 (1996): 10.

6. William E. Studwell, "Why Not an 'AACR' for Subject Headings?", *Cataloging & Classification Quarterly* 6:1 (1985): 3-9.

7. Jean Weihs, "Will the Toronto Tenets Replace the Paris Principles?", *Technicalities* 17:5 (1997): 1, 6.

8. Julia Pettee, *Subject Headings: The History and Theory of the Alphabetical Subject Approach to Books* (New York: H. W. Wilson, 1946).

9. David Judson Haykin, *Subject Headings: A Practical Guide* (Washington, D.C.: U.S. Government Printing Office, 1951).

10. Library of Congress, Subject Cataloging Manual: Subject Headings (Washington D.C.: Library of Congress, eds. of various dates, 4th ed. 1991).

11. Martha O'Hara Conway, "Library of Congress Subject Subdivisions Conference", *ALCTS Newsletter* 2 (1991): 84-86.

12. Sanford Berman, "Proposed: A Subject Code for Public, School and Community College Libraries", *HCL Cataloging Bulletin* 39 (1979): 1-5, reprinted in his

book *The Joy of Cataloging: Essays, Letters, Reviews and Other Explosions* (Phoenix: Oryx Press, 1981), p.[149]-152.

13. Lois Mai Chan, *Library of Congress Subject Headings: Principles and Application* (Littleton, Colo.: Libraries Unlimited, 1978), p. 5.

14. William E. Studwell, *Library of Congress Subject Headings: Philosophy, Practice and Prospects* (New York: Haworth Press, 1990).

15. William E. Studwell, "Who Killed the Subject Code?", *Technical Services Quarterly* 12:1 (1994): 35-41.

16. Lisa Romero, "An Evaluation of Classification and Subject Cataloging in Entry-Level Cataloging Copy: Implications for Access and Instruction", *Journal of Education for Library and Information Science* 36:3 (1995): 219.

17. Tschera Harkness Connell, "Use of the LCSH System: Realities", *Cataloging & Classification Quarterly* 23:1 (1996): 73-95.

18. Thomas Mann, "'Cataloging Must Change!' and Indexes Consistency Studies: Misreading the Evidence at Our Peril", *Cataloging & Classification Quarterly* 23:3/4 (1997): 4.

19. William E. Studwell, "Ignore It and It Will Go Away . . . But It's Still There!", *Technicalities* 17: 4 (1997): 13.

20. James R. Dwyer, "The Road to Access & the Road to Entropy", *Library Journal* 112:14 (1987): 131-136.

21. Joan M. Cherry, "Improving Subject Access in OPACs: An Exploratory Study of Conversion of Users' Queries", *Journal of Academic Librarianship* 18:2 (1992): 95-99.

22. Sanford Berman, "Arbitrary Subject Headings Assigned by the Library of Congress, or, The Importance of Alternative Cataloging-in Publication", *Librarians at Liberty* 5:2/6:1-2 (1998): 23.

23. "Digital Libraries: Global Scope, Unlimited Access", *Communications (Association for Computing Machinery)* 41:4 (1998).

24. William E. Studwell, "OPACs and the Three Multis: Looking Forward to a Possible Subject Access Environment of the Future", *Technicalities* 18:6 (1998).

25. William E. Studwell, "Universal Subject Environment: Aspirations for a Multinational, Multicultural, and Multilingual Subject Access System", *Technical Services Quarterly* 16:3 (1998).

Index

Using the Index: Most topics are in the context of the Internet and the World Wide Web, and therefore use of the terms "Internet" and "World Wide Web" as leads has been minimized. Most topics will be found directly under their names, e.g., Abstracts, Page databases, Search engines, Surfing. Where a page contains a Figure or Table, the page number is italicized, e.g., *27(Table), 117(Figure)*

T - #0542 - 101024 - C0 - 216/152/12 - PB - 9780789010315 - Gloss Lamination